# Issues in Development:
# BRAZIL

CW00792884

# Issues in Development:

# BRAZIL

Andrew Reed

UNWIN HYMAN

# Acknowledgements

The author and publishers would like to thank the following for permission to use photographs, extracts and illustrations in this book:

J. Allen Cash Limited 4.1, 4.5, 4.8, 5.6, 6.2, 6.8, 11.1, 12.4a,b,c, 12.5, 14.4, 18.4b, 20.6, 20.8, 21.3c, 21.3e, 23.6, 24.3a, 24.5a,b, 25.1; Albert Bonniers Forlag for an article from *Land and Power in South America*, p41; Steve Bowles 18.1; Brazilian Coffee Institute 12.2; Brazilian Embassy for an article from *Brazil: A Geography*, p48; Len Browne 16.5; CAFOD p89; Camera Press 1.3, 2.2, 2.5, 5.2, 6.3, 6.4, 13.2, 17.1, 17.5, 19.1a,b, 20.1, 20.3, 20.7, 24.1; Christian Aid p88, 2.4, 4.2, 15.4, 23.2, 26.1; Sue Cunningham 13.5, 18.4a, 26.4; John Dickinson 15.3, 16.3; Earth Satellite Corporation/Science Photo Library 2.1; Julio Etchart 2.3, 2.7, 4.3, 6.5, 7.1, 11.2, 16.1c, 21.3b, 22.2, 23.4, 23.5; Fiat 16.4; *Financial Times* for two extracts, pp24, 91; *Geographical Review* vol.53, 1963 for 14.1 (Taaffe, Morrill and Gould); Tom Hanley 20.4; Hutchison 5.5, 8.3, 26.5; International Coffee Organisation p83; Tom Johnston 17.6; Longman for two diagrams from *Brazil* by J. P. Dickinson, 7.5, 27.2; Tony Morrison/South American Pictures 8.4, 10.1b, 22.2, 23.7, 24.6, 27.3, 28.1; *Nature*/ Tom Johnston 17.6; *New Internationalist* p94; *Newsweek* p24; Open University 16.6; Oxfam 1.2, 9.2b, 18.4c, 21.1, 21.3d, 23.3; Pan books for 28.3, 28.4, based on *The Limits to Growth* (Meadows); Panos 1.1, 28.2; Photo Source 21.3a, 25.3; Popperfoto 5.4, 10.1a; Shell 9.2a, 16.1b; *South* Magazine for Table 1 on p52 and an article, p85; Survival International/Victor Englebert 2.6, 18.4d; Tropix 9.2c, 11.3, 11.4, 14.5, 16.1a; P. Vaughan-Williams for diagrams based on those in *Brazil* (Unwin Hyman); Wings Holidays 27.1.

Published in 1989 by
UNWIN HYMAN LIMITED
15/17 Broadwick Street
London W1V 1FP

British Library Cataloguing in Publication Data

Reed, Andrew
    Brazil.—(Issues in Development).
    1. Brazil. Economic development
    I. Title      II. Series
    330.981′063

ISBN 0 7135 2789 7

Typeset by August Filmsetting, St. Helens
Produced in Hong Kong
by Colorcraft Limited

# Contents

# Preface

**Issues in Development** is a new series of GCSE geography textbooks that provides a stimulating and up-to-date approach to the study of less developed countries. The series sets out to investigate the processes and patterns of development in three major regions of the world: Brazil, Nigeria and India. These regions are specified by examination boards in recognition of their intrinsic interest and relevance to contemporary geographical enquiry.

The books are divided into four main sections which provide a thematic framework in accordance with the national criteria for geography and GCSE syllabuses. The purpose is to promote a greater understanding and awareness of people and their environments, economic activities, regional patterns of development and the interdependent relationship between less developed and more developed countries.

The series provides a wide range of teaching resources for students of all abilities. These include case studies, extracts and reports from books and newspapers, maps, diagrams and photographs. Text and illustrations are carefully integrated with regular, structured questions and activities. The questions are broadly graded according to levels of difficulty, and designed to allow positive achievement by all students.

**Brazil** examines the major issues in the development of one of the world's largest and most rapidly developing countries. It stresses the nature, causes and consequences of Brazil's top-heavy style of development and shows how this particular case of development relates to general theories, models and principles. Among the major issues discussed in this book are the exploitation of Amazonia with the destruction of the rainforests and Indian culture, drought, poverty and migration from the North-east, contrasting wealth and opportunities in urban areas, the economic power of multinational companies and the growth of Brazil's huge foreign debt.

At the end of the book there is a data base of comparative development indicators for five countries at contrasting stages of development. The data base is designed to supplement the text and to provide information about development which may be put into a computer for graphical display and analysis. All students are encouraged to use this book in conjunction with a good atlas.

# PEOPLE AND THE ENVIRONMENT

# INDIANS ATTACK BULLDOZERS WITH BOWS AND ARROWS

With nothing but their traditional weapons – bows and poison-tipped arrows – protesting Indians try in vain to hold back the tide of progress. As the giant machines continue to forge a new road through the rainforest the Indians look all set to losing another fight against an unwanted invasion of their tribal lands. A spokesman for the construction company said he had no knowledge of local Indians living in the area. The incident would not change their plans.

▲ Fig 1
Deforestation: destruction of the rainforest and the Indian's tribal lands.

# WORLD'S LARGEST RAIN-FOREST MAY BE GONE IN 30 YEARS

There seems to be no halting the destruction of the world's largest rainforest in Amazonia. In the name of progress and development the trees, some of which take over 100 years to grow, are felled in a few minutes and burned to ashes. The soil is left exposed to the fierce tropical heat and heavy rain. The rivers here run red and yellow as precious soil is washed away leaving the ground barren and useless.

▼ Fig 2
One of Brazil's most expensive projects. Can you name it?

# BRAZIL DEBT CRISIS

Bankers meet today to discuss the world's biggest debt. Brazil has borrowed millions of dollars to help pay for much-needed development projects like the new Transamazonica Highway. But Brazil is looking for ways of delaying its repayments amid growing doubts about the environmental and human impact of many projects. It is unlikely that international banks will accept this delay.

# 1. Issues in Brazilian development

Brazil is often in the news. In Brazilian papers the reports are usually about new factories and power stations, football matches (Brazilians are football-mad) and the 'high life' in the great cities. Outside Brazil the news is different. Read the newspaper extracts opposite. They tell another story. The fact is that Brazil is changing very rapidly. But the way in which Brazil is changing has raised many important issues about the style of **development**. In its bid to develop its economic wealth, Brazil seems to have forgotten about the lives of ordinary people who are affected by the changes (Figure 3). And while foreign companies are quick to exploit Brazil's rich resources, they are very slow to show any concern for the damage that they are doing to the environment.

Use the newspaper extracts and photographs to answer these questions.

1 Give THREE reasons why Brazil is often in the news.
2 Which TWO groups of people have not benefited from Brazilian development?
3 How would you describe the speed of Brazilian development? Is it slow or rapid?
4 Brazil is still a relatively poor country. How did it pay for its development?
5 Describe TWO problems that have resulted from road-building in the rain-forests of the Amazon.
6 What do the photographs tell you about the concern being shown for ordinary people in Brazil?

▼Fig 3
Thousands of Brazilians live in home-made shacks like this one. It has no water supply or other services.

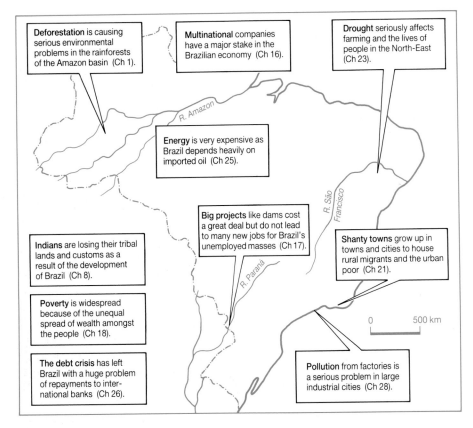

Deforestation is causing serious environmental problems in the rainforests of the Amazon basin (Ch 1).

Multinational companies have a major stake in the Brazilian economy (Ch 16).

Drought seriously affects farming and the lives of people in the North-East (Ch 23).

Energy is very expensive as Brazil depends heavily on imported oil (Ch 25).

Big projects like dams cost a great deal but do not lead to many new jobs for Brazil's unemployed masses (Ch 17).

Indians are losing their tribal lands and customs as a result of the development of Brazil (Ch 8).

Shanty towns grow up in towns and cities to house rural migrants and the urban poor (Ch 21).

Poverty is widespread because of the unequal spread of wealth amongst the people (Ch 18).

The debt crisis has left Brazil with a huge problem of repayments to international banks (Ch 26).

Pollution from factories is a serious problem in large industrial cities (Ch 28).

R. Amazon

R. São Francisco

R. Paraná

0    500 km

▲ Fig 4

## A closer look at the issues

This book looks at the main issues in Brazil's style of development. Figure 4 shows some of these issues. Study them carefully before answering the following questions.

1  Name as many issues as you can from the evidence in Figure 4.
2  Divide these issues into THREE groups using the headings:
   ENVIRONMENTAL ISSUES
   SOCIAL ISSUES
   ECONOMIC ISSUES
3  Which of these issues do you think have been caused by: (i) Brazil's links with other countries; (ii) the misuse of the environment; (iii) the unequal distribution of resources (e.g. land)?
4 a  What do you think the Brazilian government's attitude is towards development? Explain which issues demonstrate this attitude.
  b  Do you think the Brazilian government has the right attitude to the development of their country? What changes do you think should be made?

# 2. The faces of Brazil

## A satellite view of Brazil

From high up in space a photograph was taken of Brazil, using a camera mounted in a satellite. The result was the picture you can see in Figure 1. It shows two great natural features of Brazil. As the satellite passed over the Amazon region it picked up unusual heat signals. These came from huge forest fires in the jungle below. The fires were not accidental but part of the plan to clear the forest.

1 What major natural features does the satellite picture show?
2 What information did the satellite pick up about activity in Brazil?
3 Using the evidence in Figure 2, explain why the rainforests are being destroyed.

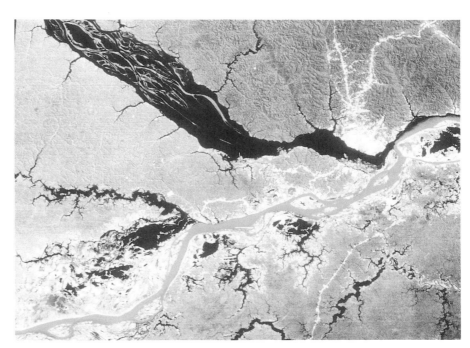

▲ Fig 1
A satellite view of Brazil above Manaus where the Rio Negro joins the Amazon river.

◀ Fig 2
Making way for a road: the destruction of the tropical rainforests of Amazonia.

## One land – two Brazils

The development of Brazil is marked by great inequalities. For all its hidden or **potential wealth**, Brazil remains a relatively poor country. The reason for this lies mainly in the Brazilian approach to development. It has been described as "top-heavy" development because emphasis is placed on the production of goods and the generation of wealth and jobs for a few rather than on improving living standards for everyone. Brazilian development has achieved remarkable economic growth rates and excellent living standards for a fortunate minority of the people. These people enjoy good housing, education and health services. For the majority of Brazilians, however, development has not solved the problems of poverty, poor housing, inadequate health care services and few schools. Low living standards are widespread in Brazil today. At the same time, Brazilian-style development has relied heavily on the rapid use or exploitation of natural resources, often without regard for the damage done to the environment and any adverse effects on the population.

So there are two major issues in Brazilian development. The first concerns the gulf in wealth, living standards and opportunities for

11

people in different parts of the country. Then there is the damage that is being done to the environment in pursuit of rapid economic growth.

Brazil is a country of such great geographical contrasts that there appear to be two Brazils. One Brazil has all the symptoms of a more developed country such as the United States (Figure 3). The other Brazil has many features in common with the less developed countries of the Third World, like neighbouring Bolivia (Figure 4).

1 a Write down the name of (i) a less developed country (LDC), and (ii) a more developed country (MDC).
  b Referring to Figures 3 and 4, describe as many symptoms of an LDC and an MDC as you can.
  c Why do you think it is difficult to say whether Brazil is a less developed or more developed country?
2 a Pick out of the text THREE pairs of words that describe different aspects of unequal development in Brazil.
  b Use these words in a short article (about 200 words) for a newspaper with the headline, 'There are two Brazils'.

◀ Fig 3
Downtown São Paulo.

▼ Fig 4
The slums of Salvador in northeast Brazil.

## Brazilian views of Brazil

People very rarely share exactly the same opinion of the place where they live. They have different views or **perceptions** of their surroundings. Here, three Brazilians tell us about their living conditions.

◄ Fig 6
Yano, a Yanomani Indian from the Amazon region.

"We are poor, like everyone here. It's a long way from the city centre but here the land is cheap, so this is where we built our hut. We've got two rooms and we just about manage. Now the authorities are saying there are too many huts on this part of the hillside and we may have to move. Nobody is prepared to say where we should go. My husband works when he can, usually on a building site. But that kind of job is irregular and the pay - well, it's not much for the hard work. The older children had to leave school early and get jobs. We can only pay for the youngest two to attend primary school. They will have to leave when they are eight. An old television - that's our only luxury. We have power cuts on about three days a week."

▲ Fig 5
Maria Rodrigues, a housewife in a favela (shanty town) in Rio de Janeiro.

"Most of our time is spent growing crops and hunting with arrows and spears. Everything we need can be found in the forest. The huts, hammocks, bows and cooking pots are made in the yano (village). We live as one large family, sharing our few possessions. Sometimes there is a great feast. We paint ourselves with black and red dyes. The worst thing for our tribe (apart from disease) is losing our land. Now we cannot hunt where white men have moved in with their new roads. We are frightened of their diseases which we cannot cure. The Father at the mission tries to teach us new things but we have our own ways. Why should we change?"

"For me Brazil is a great country. I manage a large clothes factory in São Paulo. There are so many poor people looking for jobs here that I have to turn most of them away. I go on business trips by air to Europe and North America several times each year. I take the family on holiday to somewhere interesting. Last year we went to Florida. We own a large apartment in central São Paulo. The city provides all our needs. There are good schools for our children, large air-conditioned shops, banks and places of enter-tainment. I have a Fiat car so we can drive to the hills or beaches at weekends."

◄ Fig 7
Luiz Boas, a factory manager in São Paulo.

**1 a** Judging from the three accounts, which person do you think is happiest with living conditions in Brazil?
 **b** Choose FOUR reasons from this person's account to justify your choice.
 **c** Make a list of the things the other people do not like about life in Brazil.
 **d** Using the three accounts as evidence, explain why you think Brazil has been described as having 'three faces'.

13

# 3. A question of size

## Brazil and the World

Brazil is one of the world's largest countries (Figure 1). It is far larger than any country in Western Europe. France is the largest country in Western Europe and more than twice as large as the United Kingdom. But France would fit more than 15 times into Brazil. Indeed, if the entire European Community were moved to Brazil there would still be plenty of room to spare (Figure 2). There are other ways of comparing the size of countries. Look at Table 1.

**1 a** What THREE measures of size are used in Table 1?
  **b** What is Brazil's rank in the world for each of these measures of size?
  **c** Which TWO countries rank above Brazil in each category?
**2** Make a list of the following regions in order of area: the European Community; France; Brazil; the United Kingdom; the USSR.

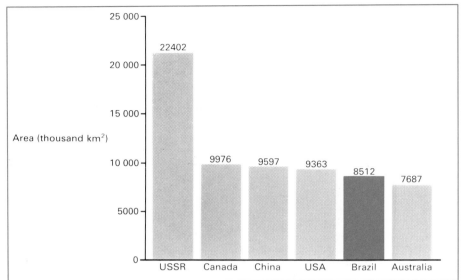

▲ Fig 1
The big six.

▼ Fig 2
The size of the European Community compared with Brazil.

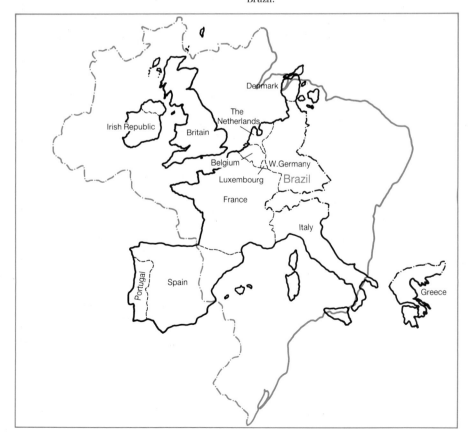

## Brazil and South America

Look carefully at the information in Figures 3 and 4.
**1** How many countries are there in South America?
**2** South America has a total population of 406,223,000. The population of each country is shown by a bar graph in Figure 3.
  **a** Work out the percentage share that each country has of the total population. Use this formula:

$$\frac{x}{y} \times 100$$

  (x = population of a country; y = population of South America).
  **b** Draw a pie graph to represent the percentages you have worked out. You will need to convert the percentages into degrees. There are 360 degrees in a circle so use this formula:

$$\frac{\%}{100} \times \frac{360}{1} \text{ OR } \% \times 3.6$$

  **c** Draw up a table to show the six leading countries of South America in rank order under the heading (i) area; (ii) population; (iii) wealth. Note that countries with the same percentages should be in the same rank.
**3** Using the rank data in your table, describe Brazil's importance in South America.

*Table 1   World ranks*

| World rank | Area | Population | Wealth |
|---|---|---|---|
| 1 | USSR | China | USA |
| 2 | Canada | India | Japan |
| 3 | China | USSR | W. Germany |
| 4 | USA | USA | France |
| 5 | **Brazil** | Indonesia | USSR |
| 6 | Australia | **Brazil** | UK |
| 7 | India | Japan | Italy |
| 8 | Argentina | Bangladesh | Canada |
| 9 | Sudan | Pakistan | **Brazil** |
| 10 | Algeria | Nigeria | Spain |

## Inside Brazil

Brazil is divided into five regions (Figure 5). Even Brazil's smallest region is larger than France. If it were a separate country, the largest Brazilian region would be the seventh largest country in the world (see Figure 6). To give some idea of the sheer size of Brazil, a journey from the north to the south of the country would be equivalent in distance to travelling from Bristol to Moscow – some 2,815 kilometres! From east to west the journey is a staggering 4,022 kilometres.

Brazil extends over a wide range of latitude and longitude because of its huge area. Very little of Brazil lies outside the tropics. This has had a significant effect upon the country's climate, vegetation and agriculture. Given its vast area, it is hardly surprising that large parts of Brazil are still unexplored and undeveloped.

1 a How many regions are there in Brazil?
  b Name the regions in order of size.
  c Which regions are larger than (i) India and (ii) Nigeria?
2 Using an atlas, work out the length of (i) Brazil's coastline and (ii) Brazil's land frontiers. (Measure with a piece of string). Your total answer (lengths (i) and (ii) added together) should come to about 23,000 km. (The exact figure is 23,121 km).
3 a Approximately what proportion of Brazil lies within the tropics (between 23.5° N and 23.5° S) (i) 50% (ii) 75% (iii) 90%?
  b Which other South American countries lie mainly in the tropics?

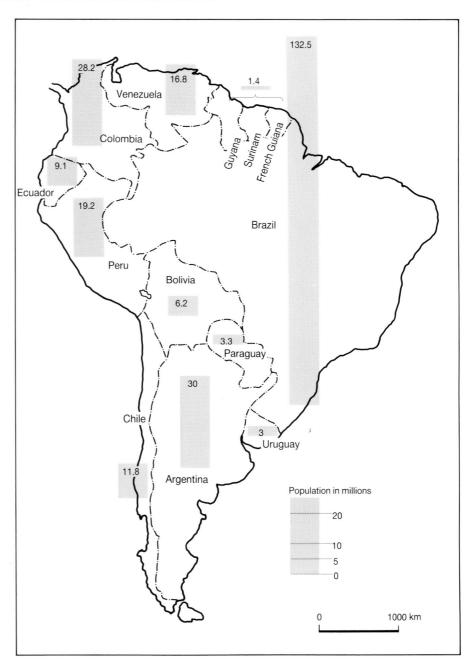

▲ Fig 3
The population of countries in South America.

15

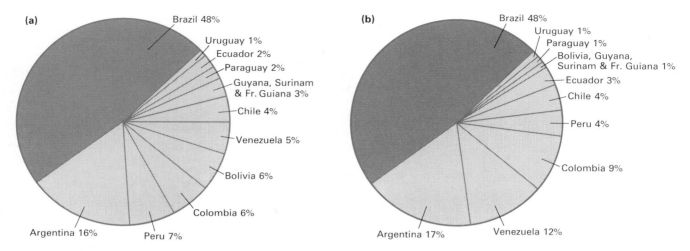

**(a)**

Brazil 48%
Uruguay 1%
Ecuador 2%
Paraguay 2%
Guyana, Surinam & Fr. Guiana 3%
Chile 4%
Venezuela 5%
Bolivia 6%
Colombia 6%
Peru 7%
Argentina 16%

**(b)**

Brazil 48%
Uruguay 1%
Paraguay 1%
Bolivia, Guyana, Surinam & Fr. Guiana 1%
Ecuador 3%
Chile 4%
Peru 4%
Colombia 9%
Venezuela 12%
Argentina 17%

▲ Fig 4
Brazil's share of
South America in
terms of (a) Area
and (b) Wealth.

▶ Fig 5
Brazil's major
regions and states.

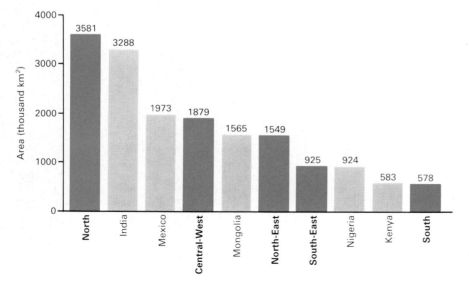

◀ Fig 6
The size of Brazil's
regions in comparison
with selected
countries.

# 4. Natural environments in Brazil

## HIGHWAY IMPASSABLE

Heavy rain and swollen rivers have covered sections of Brazil's Trans-amazonica Highway. Many vehicles have been abandoned while others await rescue.

▲ Fig 1

## NOT A DROP TO DRINK

It has not rained in the North-east for six weeks. Crops are ruined and live-stock dying. Over hundreds of square miles the drought is forcing peasants to leave the land and look for work in the towns. There is no longer any work on the farms. If they stay, then they will starve for they do not buy food – they grow it for themselves.

▲ Fig 2

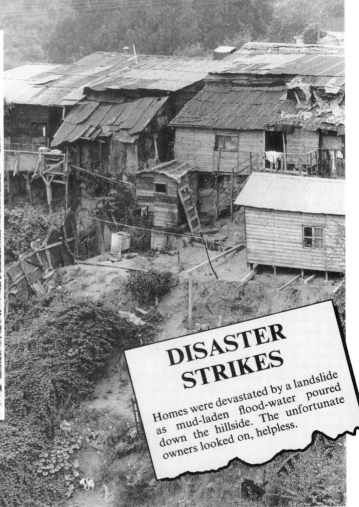

## DISASTER STRIKES

Homes were devastated by a landslide as mud-laden flood-water poured down the hillside. The unfortunate owners looked on, helpless.

▶ Fig 3

Refer to the reports of natural disasters above.

1 Name the THREE kinds of natural disaster shown in Figures 1, 2 and 3.
2 Briefly explain how people have been affected by the disaster in each case.

## The physical environment

Natural disasters such as these are quite frequent in Brazil. The lives and work of its people are affected in some way by the physical environment, though not always as dramatically as shown in the pictures on page 17. Each physical region of Brazil offers different prospects and problems for people. Read the following passage in conjunction with Figure 4.

southwards towards the coastal plain. These scarps are often formed along faults in the underlying rocks. They form a major **physical barrier** to communications with the interior of Brazil.

The lowlands of the Amazon Basin lie between the Brazilian and Guiana Highlands. Here there is a huge

sedimentary basin made up of deposits laid down by the Amazon River. The Amazon is rapidly eroding the highlands in the upper reaches of the river system. In the lower reaches there is rapid deposition of river material called **alluvium**. It is estimated that the Amazon carries a load of 1.3 million tonnes of sediment each day.'

(Adapted from *Brazil: A Geography*)

1 Name the FOUR major physical regions of Brazil.
2 Look carefully at Figure 5. Which physical region is shown in the photograph? Give reasons for your answer.
3 Explain the following terms used in the passage: (i) shield area; (ii) physical barrier; (iii) alluvium.

▼ Fig 4
The main physical regions of Brazil.

Mountain ranges
Escarpments
Amazon Basin
Guiana Highlands
Coastal Strip
Brazilian Highlands Central Plateau
Major river system

R. Amazon

R. São Francisco

R. Paraná

0    500 km

## Climatic conditions

Although Brazil lies largely within the tropics, it experiences a considerable range of climatic conditions. The most striking differences are between northern, north-eastern and southern Brazil.

Study the rainfall map (Figure 6), the climate graphs (Figure 7) and the climate data in Table 1 carefully.

▼ Fig 5
Note the physical setting of Rio de Janeiro.

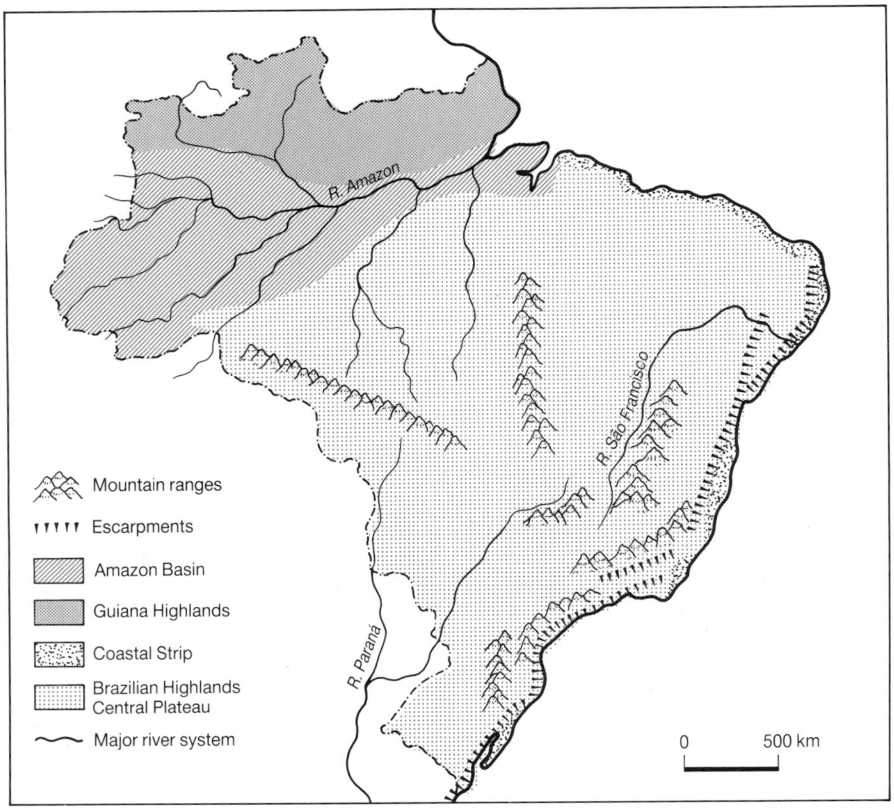

'Almost half of Brazil's territory consists of plains and lowlands: the Amazon Basin in the north, the narrow coastal strip running from the north-east to Rio de Janeiro and the basin of the River Plate in the south. The rest of the territory consists of the Brazilian Highlands, the vast Central Plateau and the Guiana Highlands, north of the Amazon.

The plateaux are part of the ancient **shield area** of South America. They are made up of ancient crystalline rocks which are among the oldest in the world. The rocks of the shield areas are rich in minerals such as iron ore, nickel, lead and gold. With such extensive shield areas it is not surprising that Brazil has huge mineral reserves.

The Brazilian Highlands form sharp ridges or **escarpments** in the south-east with the steep scarp slope facing

1 For each climate station calculate
  a the range of temperature (highest temperature − lowest temperature);
  b the annual rainfall.
  c the amount of rainfall at Quixeramobim and São Gabriel from (i) Jan−June and (ii) July−December.
  d Using this information, describe the different rainfall regimes or patterns at these two places.
2 a Using the data in Table 1, draw temperature and rainfall graphs for São Paulo. They should be drawn to the same scale as Figure 7.
  b Compare your climate graphs with the two graphs in Figure 7. Which climate station shows (i) high temperatures all year; (ii) the highest summer temperatures; (iii) a marked hot and cool season; (iv) rainfall all year; (v) a long dry season?
3 The climate stations are represented on Figure 6 by the letters X, Y and Z. Match each letter with the appropriate place.

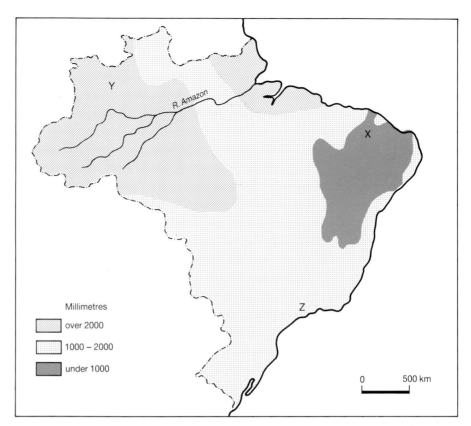

▶ Fig 6
Average annual rainfall.

Millimetres
over 2000
1000 – 2000
under 1000

0    500 km

Table 1  Climate data

**Temperature in °C**

|  | Jan | Feb | March | April | May | June | July | Aug | Sept | Oct | Nov | Dec | Mean |
|---|---|---|---|---|---|---|---|---|---|---|---|---|---|
| São Gabriel | 25.4 | 25.6 | 25.5. | 25.2 | 25.0 | 24.5 | 24.3 | 24.8 | 25.4 | 25.6 | 25.9 | 25.4 | 25.2 |
| Quixeramobim | 28.8 | 27.9 | 27.0 | 27.0 | 26.5 | 26.1 | 26.6 | 27.6 | 28.2 | 28.5 | 28.6 | 29.0 | 27.6 |
| São Paulo | 20.8 | 20.9 | 20.6 | 18.8 | 16.6 | 15.4 | 14.9 | 15.5 | 16.3 | 17.5 | 18.5 | 20.1 | 18.0 |

**Rainfall in mm**

|  | Jan | Feb | March | April | May | June | July | Aug | Sept | Oct | Nov | Dec | Total |
|---|---|---|---|---|---|---|---|---|---|---|---|---|---|
| São Gabriel | 269 | 222 | 261 | 247 | 305 | 232 | 227 | 207 | 151 | 166 | 194 | 303 | — |
| Quixeramobim | 42 | 121 | 209 | 173 | 118 | 58 | 16 | 5 | 6 | 3 | 4 | 10 | — |
| São Paulo | 215 | 175 | 161 | 77 | 65 | 40 | 24 | 48 | 92 | 121 | 138 | 188 | — |

▼ Fig 7
Climate data:
(a) Rainfall
(b) Temperature.

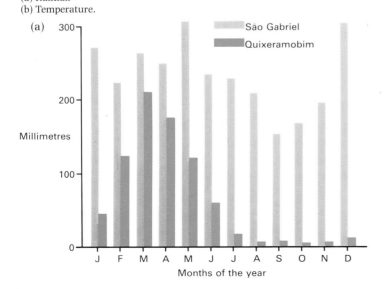

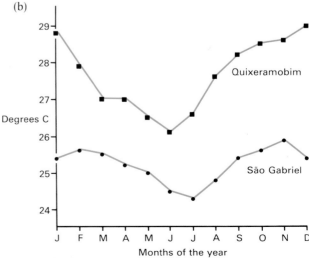

◀Fig 8
Water power: the Iguaçu Falls in Paraná State.

▼Fig 9
The hydrology of three Brazilian river systems.

In the north of Brazil there are no seasons as the weather is hot and humid all year. This region has an **equatorial climate**. North-eastern Brazil experiences these conditions for part of the year only. During the winter months (June to November), the equatorial low pressure system moves northwards, making way for the tropical high pressure system. As the pressure systems move, the hot, humid, rainy summer weather gives way to slightly cooler but very dry winter conditions. In contrast to the **tropical climate** of the north-east, southern Brazil has a **temperate climate**. Here the difference between summer and winter temperatures is more marked. Frosts occur every winter in the extreme south, but even here the average annual temperature is 17° C, considerably higher than anywhere in Britain.

1 a What type of climate would you find at: (i) São Paulo; (ii) São Gabriel and (iii) Quixeramobim?
  b In which parts of Brazil are these climatic conditions found?
2 Imagine you are advising a friend who is about to visit Brazil. Describe the kind of weather your friend can expect: (i) on arriving in São Paulo in July; (ii) on a visit to relatives in north-east Brazil in August; (iii) on a sight-seeing trip to see the Amazon in December.
3 In which climatic region would you expect to experience (i) droughts; (ii) seasonal floods and (iii) sub-zero temperatures? Provide clear reasons, with facts from this chapter to support your answers.

## River systems

Rivers like the Iguaçu (Figure 8) have played a vital part in the development of Brazil. For early settlers, travel by river was often the only way of penetrating inland because there were no roads or railways. Today, rivers are more important for supplying energy (hydro-electric power) and irrigation than for transport. However, because of their different patterns of water flow or **hydrology**, each of the main rivers is quite distinctive. Study the information on the three river systems in Figure 9. (You will find the rivers marked on Figure 4).

1 a Name the three major rivers of Brazil.
  b Which river system: (i) is the largest in Brazil? (ii) lies entirely in Brazil? (iii) drains southwards? (iv) rises in Peru?
2 Which river is likely to be most important for irrigation? Give reasons for your answer. (Consult the rainfall map in Figure 6).
3 Compare the hydrological characteristics of the Amazon and São Francisco rivers. Using the information in this chapter, explain the differences you have noted.

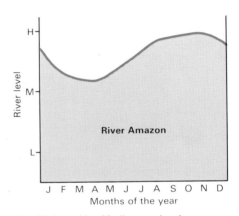

H = High    M = Medium    L = Low

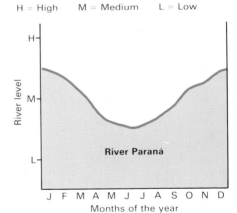

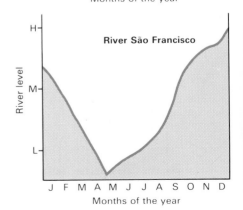

# 5. Land for a living

## Ecosystems at work

The tropical rainforests of Brazil are rapidly being destroyed. They are being cleared for timber and to make way for roads, mines, farms and ranches. Some people call this development. However, the destruction of the rainforests is causing a major environmental

**d** Why will plants no longer grow in an unstable ecosystem?

**3** Carbon dioxide ($CO_2$) in the atmosphere absorbs heat energy from the sun. It acts like a filter, so the temperature does not rise too high. Large areas of forest produce a great deal of $CO_2$. What effect might large-scale deforestation have on the temperature of the atmosphere?

**4** Referring to Figures 1 and 2, explain the main differences between a stable and an unstable ecosystem.

**5 a** Why do you think the destruction of the rainforests is sometimes taken as a sign of development?

**b** Do you agree with this view? Give your reasons.

## Major natural environments

People depend on the environment for supplies of food and water. Not all areas of land have the same potential for food production because of different environmental conditions. Apart from a relatively small temperate region in the extreme south, Brazil is a land of tropical environments which vary according to physical conditions. The major

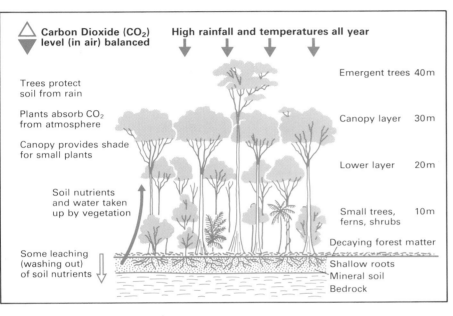

**Carbon Dioxide ($CO_2$) level (in air) balanced**

**High rainfall and temperatures all year**

Trees protect soil from rain

Plants absorb $CO_2$ from atmosphere

Canopy provides shade for small plants

Soil nutrients and water taken up by vegetation

Some leaching (washing out) of soil nutrients

Emergent trees 40m

Canopy layer 30m

Lower layer 20m

Small trees, ferns, shrubs 10m

Decaying forest matter

Shallow roots
Mineral soil
Bedrock

◀ Fig 1
The rainforest – a stable ecosystem.

▼ Fig 2
After deforestation – an unstable ecosystem.

problem. But why should felling trees cause problems? The fact is that the rainforests are part of a finely-balanced system known as an **ecosystem**. Look at Figure 1. It explains how the rainforest ecosystem works. If one part of the system is changed then there is a 'knock-on' effect somewhere else in the system. Cutting down trees on a large scale throws the rainforest ecosystem out of balance. It becomes unstable. The effect on the environment can be dramatic (Figure 2).

**1 a** Name FOUR main inputs in the rainforest ecosystem.

**b** How many layers of vegetation are there in the rainforest?

**c** Explain the effect of these layers on temperatures and rainfall at ground level.

**2 a** Name TWO kinds of plant nutrient or food in the soil.

**b** How is the fertility of the soil maintained?

**c** What major change in the ecosystem is shown in Figure 2?

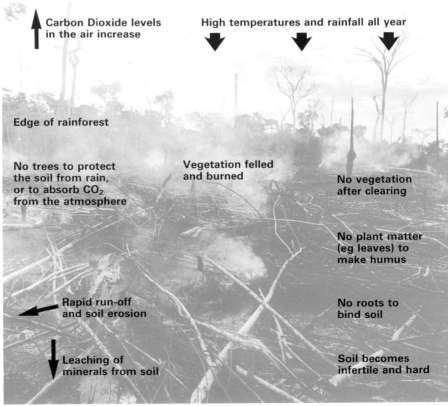

**Carbon Dioxide levels in the air increase**

**High temperatures and rainfall all year**

Edge of rainforest

No trees to protect the soil from rain, or to absorb $CO_2$ from the atmosphere

Vegetation felled and burned

No vegetation after clearing

No plant matter (eg leaves) to make humus

Rapid run-off and soil erosion

No roots to bind soil

Leaching of minerals from soil

Soil becomes infertile and hard

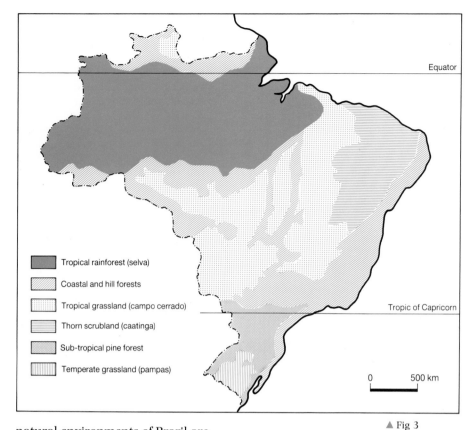

Tropical rainforest (selva)

Coastal and hill forests

Tropical grassland (campo cerrado)

Thorn scrubland (caatinga)

Sub-tropical pine forest

Temperate grassland (pampas)

Equator

Tropic of Capricorn

0    500 km

## Tropical grasslands

Tropical grasslands, known as **campo cerrado** in Brazil, cover much of the interior to the south of the rainforests (Figure 5). The long dry season and regular burning by Indians in the past have helped maintain this ecosystem. The practice of bush-burning is very common as it encourages new grass and discourages tree growth. The soils in this region are generally very poor, lacking in plant nutrients such as humus. The cerrado, like the selva, is easily degraded and turned into a desert if the ecosystem is upset. As a result, the potential for agriculture is limited unless modern scientific farming methods are used to improve the soil with fertilizers and irrigation.

## Thorn scrubland

In north-east Brazil the long dry season has a marked effect upon the natural vegetation. Plants have adapted themselves to the high

▲ Fig 3
Major natural environments in Brazil.

▼ Fig 4
How many layers of vegetation can you detect?

natural environments of Brazil are shown in Figure 3. Tropical rainforests, grasslands and scrublands cover over 95 per cent of Brazil.

## The rainforests

The rainforests or **selva** occupy five million square kilometres in South America. Over 80 per cent of these rainforests are in Brazil (Figure 4). Unlike the coniferous forests in temperate latitudes, the selva contains a great variety of broadleaf evergreen trees, including valuable hardwoods like teak. The forest is arranged in layers as plants struggle to reach the light. The luxuriant growth of plants is due to the continuous growing season and constantly hot, humid climate. The selva is not only rich in plant life. There are over 8,600 species of birds, over 1,500 species of fish and numerous animals such as the sloth and anteater. Until the arrival of Europeans in Brazil over four hundred years ago, the forest was largely unchanged by man. The selva had been the home of Indians long before Europeans arrived in Brazil. Their way of life did not involve destruction of the forest environment and so the ecosystem was not upset.

▲ Fig 5
What is the main type of vegetation here?

► Fig 6
What does this vegetation tell you about the climate?

1 Study the main types of natural vegetation in Figures 4, 5 and 6.
   a What are they called?
   b Which type has the widest variety of plants and animals?
   c Describe THREE ways in which people have upset the ecosystems in Brazil.
2 Make a tracing of Figure 3. Place this over the map of rainfall (Figure 6 on page 19). Using this information and the climatic data in Table 1 on page 19, describe the seasonal pattern of temperature and rainfall for the three major natural environments of Brazil.
3 a Name THREE consequences of deforestation.
   b State whether desertification in Brazil is caused by natural or human processes.
   c How do you think desertification can be halted?
4 If you were an environmental adviser to the Brazilian Government, what advice would you give the Government on the need for the conservation of the rainforests?

temperatures and low rainfall of the region (Figure 6). Such plants are drought-resistant or *xerophytic*. The thorn scrub of this region is known as the **caatinga**.

## From green hell to red desert

The tropical rainforests of Brazil are sometimes called the 'green hell' because they appear so inhospitable to people. They have also been called the Wild West and the Last Frontier of Brazil. This view implies that the rainforests are there to be conquered and overcome. At present the spread of large-scale forestry, farming and cattle ranching in the selva, cerrado and caatinga regions is taking place without any consideration of the environmental cost. These regions are slowly being turned into deserts. The process of **desertification** leaves the land infertile and useless for agriculture. Unsuitable kinds of development and the mismanagement of the ecosystems are the main causes of desertification in Brazil.

# 6. Resources for a living

## A new paradise?

When the Portuguese discovered Brazil they thought they had found a paradise of untold wealth. They called it El Dorado, the land of gold. Brazil has lived up to the expectations of the early European explorers. In terms of **natural resources**, Brazil ranks as one of the richest countries in the world.

## Case study 1: Wealth under the ground

At the heart of the struggle for the Amazon are some of nature's most dazzling unclaimed prizes. Beneath the dense tropical growth of the eastern Amazon lies enough high-grade iron ore to meet world demand for four centuries. The jungle covers immense concentrations of bauxite, the reddish ore that is refined to make aluminium. Vast reserves of gold, nickel, copper, tin and timber sit untapped in the rainforest … (Figure 1)
(*Newsweek*, 25 January 1982)

The reserves at Carajas are estimated at 18 billion tonnes; it is the largest concentration of high-grade iron ore discovered to date in the world.
In the Amazon region, known reserves of bauxite total 46 billion tonnes. This is just the tip of Brazil's mineral iceberg; now important deposits of tin have been discovered at Pitinga – important because these reserves should yield 20,000 tonnes annually for 30 years and the current price of tin is around $7,500 a tonne. (Figure 2)

## Gold rush in Brazil

As soon as gold was discovered at Serra Pelada in 1980 thousands of men swarmed into the great open mines armed only with spades or their bare hands [Figure 3]. They are paid according to how much gold they find. Many diggers have fallen to their deaths in deep mud pools and underneath landslides of earth and rock.

| | |
|---|---|
| Fe | Iron ore |
| o | Limestone and Dolomite |
| Au | Gold |
| S | Salt |
| Mn | Manganese |
| D● | Diamonds and gemstones |
| Al | Bauxite |
| Pb | Lead |
| Cr | Chromium |
| Sn | Tin |
| Cu | Copper |
| Ni | Nickel |

1 Carajás (Fe Mn)
2 Trombetas (Al)
3 Corumba (Fe Mn)
4 Patos de Minas (Phosphates)
5 Pitinga (Sn)
6 Serra Pelada (Au)

Iron quadrilateral of Minas Gerais

► Iron Ore Terminals

0    500 km

▲ Fig 1
The main mining areas of Brazil.

◄ Fig 2
A tin mine in Amazonia. How do you think they obtain the tin?

▼ Fig 3
Gold Rush! The Serra Pelada gold mine, Para. What kind of a living is this?

The traditional mining region in Brazil lies in the state of Minas Gerais (Figure 4). Yet recent discoveries of minerals in the Amazon Basin now show that other parts of the country have even greater mineral resources.

## Case study 2: Power from rivers

Brazil's rivers are a major source of natural energy (Figure 5). The potential is vast. Although it is the largest river system in Brazil, the Amazon could provide less than 10 per cent of Brazil's potential water-power. The Amazon and its one

▲ Fig 4
Open-cast iron ore mining at Itabira in Minas Gerais.

hundred years to reach full size, getting them to regenerate by planting new trees is a very slow process. These hardwoods are very valuable because they only grow within the rainforest region, and the timber is in great demand in countries like Britain and the USA. In the south of Brazil there are forests of **softwood** trees, especially the Paraná pine. This softwood is exploited for timber, pulp and paper-making. These trees grow relatively quickly – about twenty years for a pine – so it is easier to maintain stocks of softwood. Over 50 per cent of Brazil's forestry occurs in the South, compared to less than 10 per cent in Amazonia.

1 a What is the meaning of 'El Dorado'?
  b What are the 'dazzling unclaimed prizes' described in the section 'Wealth under the ground'?
2 Referring to the maps and photographs, name FIVE examples of major natural resources in Brazil.
3 a Name THREE methods of mining in Brazil.
  b Why do you think mining at Serra Pelada is a dangerous job?

▲ Fig 5
The Itaipu hydro-electric power station – one of the largest in the world.

hundred major tributaries flow too slowly to be very suitable for hydro-electric power production. There is much more potential energy in Brazil's other major rivers (Figure 6). However, many of the best sites for HEP stations are a long distance from the large centres of population and industry. This factor has hindered the development of HEP. But for development in the future, water power is all the more valuable because Brazil has few other natural sources of energy such as oil.

## Case study 3: Timber!

Brazil is a land of forests (Figure 7). The selva contains over four hundred species of commercially useful **hardwood** timber like teak and mahogany (Figure 8). These trees do not grow together in stands, but alone as single trees. Because of this, hardwood trees are costly to exploit. Also, as large trees may take over a

▼ Fig 6
Brazil's hydro-electric power resources.

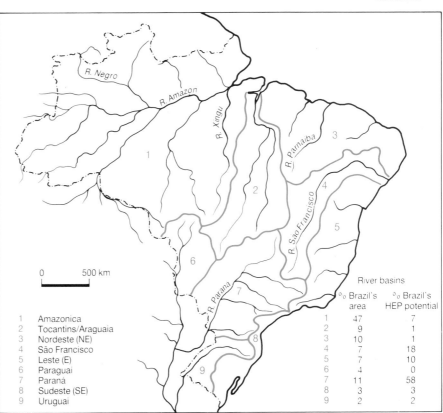

| | River basins | |
| --- | --- | --- |
| | % Brazil's area | % Brazil's HEP potential |
| 1 Amazonica | 47 | 7 |
| 2 Tocantins/Araguaia | 9 | 1 |
| 3 Nordeste (NE) | 10 | 1 |
| 4 São Francisco | 7 | 18 |
| 5 Leste (E) | 7 | 10 |
| 6 Paraguai | 4 | 0 |
| 7 Paraná | 11 | 58 |
| 8 Sudeste (SE) | 3 | 3 |
| 9 Uruguai | 2 | 2 |

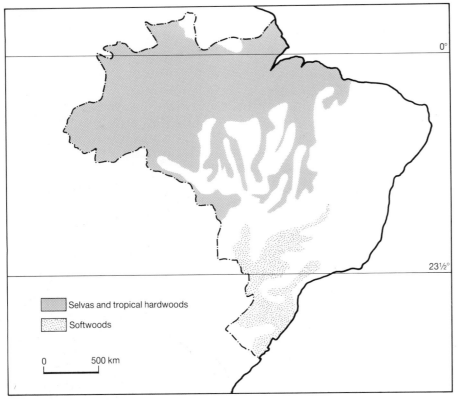

Selvas and tropical hardwoods

Softwoods

0   500 km

new deposits have to be discovered elsewhere. The search for minerals helps to establish what are called **known reserves**, that is, supplies which may be tapped in the future.

## Exploitation and conservation

Brazil is faced with choices over the **exploitation** of its vast natural resources. It wants to unlock this potential and turn it into wealth. At the same time there is growing concern for the environment as big businesses destroy the rainforests in order to get at the resources. In the past it was said that **conservation** was a luxury that Brazil could not afford. Now environmental experts are saying that the exploitation of the rainforests is having a disastrous effect. The fact is that companies want short-term profits. They are not

◄ Fig 7
Brazil's forest resources.

▼ Fig 9
A classification of natural resources.

4 a In what way are rivers a major natural resource?
  b Write out TWO lists showing Brazil's river basins in order of (i) size, and (ii) percentage of HEP potential.
  c Using the information in this chapter, explain why the order of river basins in your two lists is different.
  d Imagine you are an engineer who has been asked to recommend a site for a new HEP station in Brazil. You have to choose between possible sites on the Paraná and Parnaiba rivers. Make your recommendation, giving reasons for your choice.
5 a Name TWO important differences between hardwood and softwood trees.
  b Which forests are most heavily exploited?
  c What problems must be faced in the development of forestry in Amazonia?

```
                    Natural resources
                   /                \
        Renewable resources      Non-renewable resources
         /          \                      |
Biological      Physical              Physical
resources       resources             resources
  /    \         /    |    \            /      \
Plants  Soils  Water  Sun   Wind    Minerals  Fossil fuels
(eg trees,     power (solar power            (coal, gas and oil)
grass)              energy)
```

## Natural resources

One way of classifying natural resources is shown in Figure 9. **Biological resources** consist of plants which by their nature are renewable, as plants can regenerate from seeds. But potentially renewable resources like timber can be destroyed by exploitation if the ecosystem in which they belong is damaged. Some **physical resources** are also renewable, like water power and solar energy which can be harnessed to provide electricity. Not all energy resources are renewable. Fossil fuels, that is coal, gas and oil, run out like any other mineral. Most physical resources like minerals are non-renewable. Once a mineral like iron ore has been extracted from a mine,

interested in the long-term conservation of resources. But conservation makes sound environmental and economic sense. It means that some resources, like minerals, will last longer. Others, like trees, would not be lost for ever.

1 Which of the resources shown in Figures 2, 3, 4, 5 and 8 are: (i) renewable and (ii) non-renewable?
2 a Explain the difference between these two groups of natural resources.
  b Into which category would you place the following natural resources: gold, mahogany, rubber, iron ore, oil, wind, gas, pine trees, solar energy, rivers?
3 Make TWO lists giving as many reasons as you can find in this section in favour of (i) the conservation and (ii) the exploitation of the rainforests of Amazonia.

◄ Fig 8
Wealth from the rainforests: mahogany timber being transported in Amazonia.

# 7. Opening up Brazil

▲Fig 1
A street in the banking
district of São Paulo.

▼Fig 2
The advance of
settlement in Brazil.

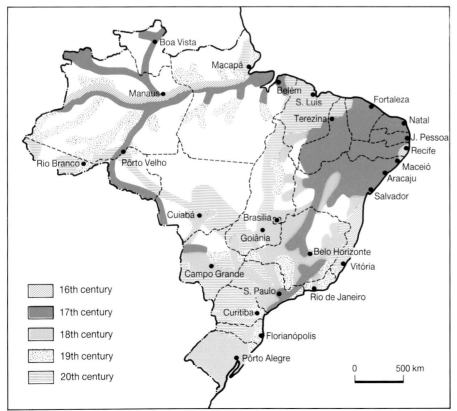

16th century
17th century
18th century
19th century
20th century

0        500 km

## Exploration and colonization

Look at the photograph in Figure 1
and notice the number of different
races to be found in Brazil. How has
this mix of races come about? The
discovery of Vera Cruz by Portuguese
seamen under Pedro Alvares Cabral
in 1500 marked the start of **European
influence** which changed the face of
the country that was later named
Brazil. But the Age of Discovery did
not signal the beginning of Brazilian
development; the Europeans had
discovered a country that was already
inhabited! Indians had lived in
scattered tribal groups for over 3,000
years before the arrival of Cabral. But
the arrival of Europeans started what
may be called the **colonial phase** of
Brazilian development. With such a
huge territory and formidable barriers
like the rainforests of the Amazon
basin, it is hardly surprising that the
small number of white settlers had
not explored or settled large areas of
Brazil by the time of **independence** in
1822.

Study Figure 2 carefully. It shows the advance of settlement in Brazil from the arrival of the Portuguese in the sixteenth century.

1 Which parts of Brazil were settled during the following periods: (i) sixteenth century; (ii) seventeenth century; (iii) eighteenth century; (iv) nineteenth century?

2 a Give the dates of the colonial period in Brazil.

   b Approximately what proportion of Brazil was settled by colonists in 1822 (i) 25% (ii) 50% (iii) 80%?

   c Why do you think the occupation of all parts of Brazil by white settlers was incomplete at the end of the colonial period?

3 Find THREE reasons for the uneven pattern of settlement in Brazil during the colonial period.

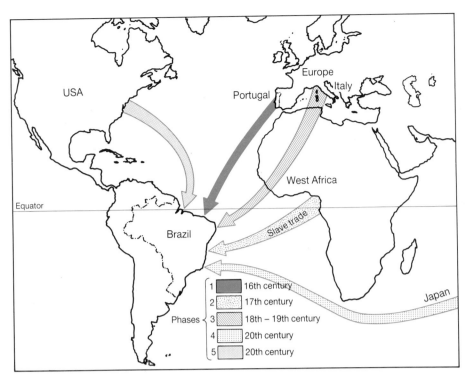

▲ Fig 3
Phases of immigration in Brazil.

## The Brazilians

Five hundred years ago Brazil was unknown to the West. It was populated by tribal Indians who belong to a similar **ethnic group** to the North American Indians and the Eskimo. Today Brazil is a multi-ethnic nation with people who originally

▼ Fig 4
Immigration to Brazil and São Paulo State, 1880–1939.

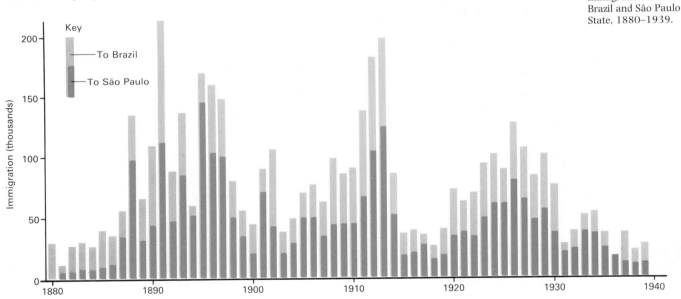

came from Europe, Africa, Asia and North America. Figure 3 shows how Brazil became populated by people from these continents. For most **immigrants** it was a question of work. Not all came willingly. Many slaves were brought in from Africa by the Portuguese landowners to work on the sugar plantations in north-east Brazil. After independence it was mainly Italians and Japanese who came to Brazil to work on the coffee

plantations in São Paulo State. Many people from European countries settled in southern Brazil as they were accustomed to living in a temperate climate. However, laws were passed in the 1930s to restrict immigration. The government also passed laws to control the type of people entering the country. They wanted to make sure that most immigrants were farmers in order to build up a skilled rural workforce.

There has been much intermarriage between the different racial groups. This is one reason why Brazil is remarkably free of **racial intolerance**. The last census which recorded the colour of Brazilian skins was taken in 1950. It showed that whites made up 62% of the population, blacks 11% and browns 27%. Portuguese is the language spoken by all Brazilians except for some remote Indian tribes.

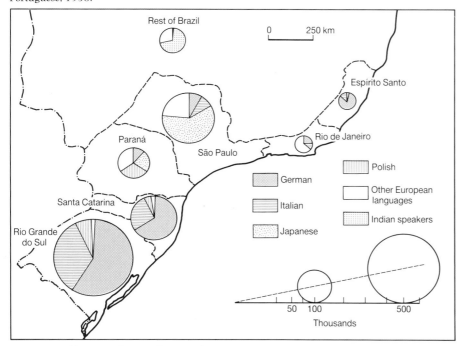

▼Fig 5
The distribution of people whose first language was not Portuguese, 1950.

Rest of Brazil

0    250 km

Espírito Santo

Paraná

Rio de Janeiro

São Paulo

German

Italian

Japanese

Polish

Other European languages

Indian speakers

Santa Catarina

Rio Grande do Sul

50  100       500
Thousands

Source: *Brazil* by J.P. Dickenson (Longman)

1 Who were the original inhabitants of Brazil?
2 Name FIVE countries or regions from which immigrants came to Brazil.
3 Draw a pie graph showing the relative sizes of Brazil's major ethnic groups in 1950.
4 Study Figure 4, which shows the annual rate of immigration into Brazil and the state of São Paulo in south-east Brazil.
  a Name THREE peak years for immigration into Brazil.
  b In which years did the rate of immigration into Brazil exceed 150,000 people?
  c Why did immigration to Brazil decline after 1930?
  d How do you account for the high proportion of immigrants in São Paulo State?
5 Refer to the information in Figure 5.
  a Account for the popularity of the southern states of Brazil for European immigrants.
  b Why do you think there is a concentration of Japanese and Italian immigrants in the state of São Paulo?

# 8. Population

## The population explosion

Most developing countries are experiencing rapid **population growth**. It is so fast in comparison with population growth in more developed countries that it is sometimes called the population explosion (Figure 1). Figures 1–4 illustrate some of the main features of Brazil's population. Study them carefully.

**1** Make a list of at least FOUR features of Brazil's population, using the evidence in Figures 1–4.

**2 a** Which nation, Brazil or the UK, had the larger population in (i) 1871; (ii) 1981?

**b** In which decade did Brazil and the UK have a similar population?

**3 a** Using the graph in Figure 1, work out the approximate population of Brazil in the following years: (i) 1871; (ii) 1905; (iii) 1939; (iv) 1965; (v) 1981.

**b** The number of years it takes for a population to double itself is called the 'doubling time'. What was the doubling time for Brazil's population in (i) 1905; (ii) 1939 and (iii) 1965?

**4 a** Make a tracing of the map of Brazil on page 16.

**b** Referring to Table 1 for the data, draw a population density map of Brazil. Use the population density groups and style of shading provided in this key:

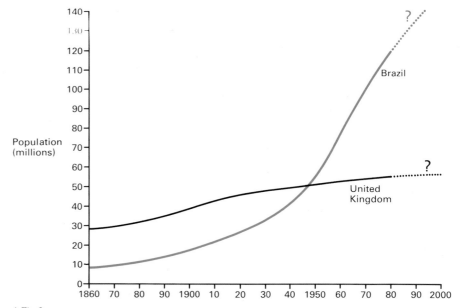

▲ Fig 1
Brazil's population explosion.

**c** Write down the names of THREE regions that have: (i) a high population density and (ii) a low population density.

**d** Using information provided in earlier chapters, find at least FIVE reasons for the uneven distribution of Brazil's population.

Persons per km²

| | |
|---|---|
| | 0 – 5 |
| | 6 – 20 |
| | 21 – 80 |
| | Over 81 |

► Fig 3
In the city, families with only two children are not uncommon.

► Fig 4
A rural family in north-east Brazil.

▼ Fig 2
The move from country to city.

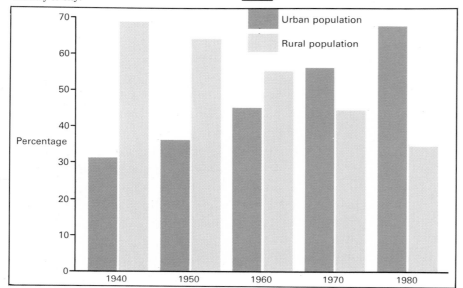

Urban population

Rural population

Percentage

1940    1950    1960    1970    1980

**5 a** Using the information in Figure 2, work out the proportion of Brazilians living in rural areas in (i) 1940; (ii) 1950; (iii) 1960; (iv) 1970 and (v) 1980.

**b** What effect is the move to cities having on the distribution of population in Brazil?

*Table 1  Population density in Brazil, 1981*

| State | Area (km²) | Population | Density |
|---|---|---|---|
| NORTH | 3,581,180 | 7,074,000 | 2 |
| Rondônia | 243,044 | 688,000 | 3 |
| Acre | 152,589 | 348,000 | 2 |
| Amazonas | 1,564,445 | 1,674,000 | 1 |
| Roraima | 230,104 | 99,000 | 0 |
| Pará | 1,250,722 | 4,058,000 | 3 |
| Amapá | 140,276 | 207,000 | 1 |
| NORTH-EAST | 1,548,672 | 38,369,000 | 25 |
| Maranhão | 328,663 | 4,525,000 | 14 |
| Piaui | 250,934 | 2,378,000 | 9 |
| Ceará | 150,630 | 5,785,000 | 38 |
| Rio Grande do Norte | 53,015 | 2,085,000 | 39 |
| Paraiba | 56,372 | 2,971,000 | 53 |
| Pernambuco | 98,281 | 6,662,000 | 68 |
| Alagoas | 27,731 | 2,199,000 | 79 |
| Fernando de Noronha* | 26 | 1,279 | 49 |
| Sergipe | 21,994 | 1,260,000 | 57 |
| Bahia | 561,026 | 10,504,000 | 19 |
| SOUTH-EAST | 924,935 | 57,942,000 | 63 |
| Minas Gerais | 587,172 | 14,381,000 | 24 |
| Esperito Santo | 45,597 | 2,239,000 | 49 |
| Rio de Janeiro | 44,268 | 12,502,000 | 282 |
| São Paulo | 247,898 | 28,820,000 | 116 |
| SOUTH | 577,723 | 20,363,000 | 35 |
| Paraná | 199,554 | 7,994,000 | 40 |
| Santa Catarina | 95,985 | 4,011,000 | 42 |
| Rio Grande do Sul | 282,184 | 8,358,000 | 30 |
| CENTRAL WEST | 1,879,455 | 8,832,000 | 5 |
| Mato Grosso | 881,001 | 1,418,000 | 2 |
| Mato Grosso do Sul | 350,548 | 1,562,000 | 4 |
| Goiás | 642,092 | 4,347,000 | 7 |
| Distrito Federal* | 5,814 | 1,505,000 | 259 |

*Too small to include in Figure 5 (Chapter 3).

## Many young and few old

Most Brazilian families are large. For a mother to have five or six children is not unusual, especially in rural areas. Large families are less common in the big cities. The need for many children to help work on the land does not apply to the peasant farmers who have moved to the city. The priorities for these **rural migrants** are likely to be education and finding jobs. So Brazil's population growth rate is slowing down (Table 2). Even so, compared to more developed countries like the UK, Brazil still has a very youthful population. The structure of Brazil's population is shown by a **population pyramid** (Figure 5). Brazil's population is 'bottom heavy' in contrast to the 'top heavy' population structure of a more developed country like the UK.

The **demographic transition model** shows how birth and death rates change over time (Figure 6). This model can be used to predict future population growth by showing the way in which birth and death rates are expected to decline. These changes are mainly brought about by improved health services and standards of living. People live longer as **life expectancy** is increased by safer and healthier living conditions.

**1** To work out the rate of population growth subtract the death rate from the birth rate and divide the result by 10. The answer is shown as a percentage, e.g. 3.1%.

  **a** Calculate the rate of Brazil's population growth in (i) 1960; (ii) 1970; (iii) 1980 and (iv) 1985 using the data in Table 2.

▼ Fig 5
The age and sex structure of the population of Brazil and the UK.

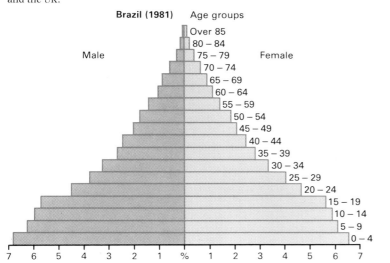

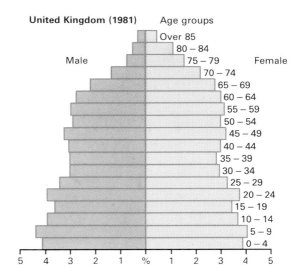

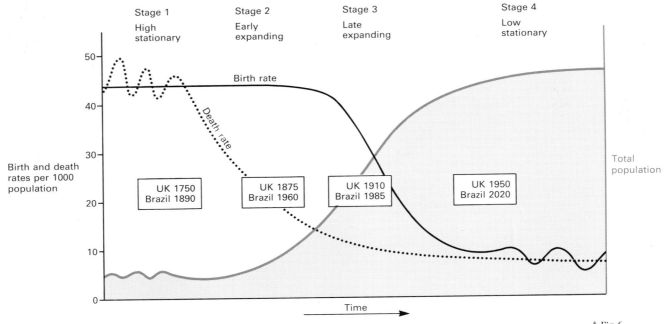

Stage 1
High stationary

Stage 2
Early expanding

Stage 3
Late expanding

Stage 4
Low stationary

Birth and death rates per 1000 population

Birth rate

Death rate

UK 1750
Brazil 1890

UK 1875
Brazil 1960

UK 1910
Brazil 1985

UK 1950
Brazil 2020

Total population

Time

▲ Fig 6
The demographic transition model.

Table 2   Birth and death rates, 1960–1985

| | Rate per '000 population | | | | | |
| | 1960 | 1965 | 1970 | 1975 | 1980 | 1985 |
|---|---|---|---|---|---|---|
| Birth rate | 43 | 39 | 36 | 33 | 31 | 30 |
| Death rate | 13 | 10 | 9 | 9 | 8.5 | 8 |

b State how the rate of increase has changed between 1960 and 1985.

2 a Draw two bar graphs showing (i) birth and (ii) death rates in Table 2. Label the scales on the x and y axes (rates and years). Give your graphs a title.

b Which stage of the demographic transition (Figure 6) did the population of Brazil correspond to in (i) 1960 and (ii) 1985?

3 a Study Figure 5. Describe the main differences between the population structures of Brazil and the United Kingdom.

b How do you account for the differences you have noted?

## Case study: The Indian population crisis

While the population of Brazil as a whole has grown rapidly, the number of Indians has declined drastically in the last four hundred years. The Tupi-speaking tribes of the north-east coastal regions were killed by early Portuguese settlers in the sixteenth century. The Omagua and Tapajos Indians who lived on the banks of the Amazon river were wiped out by the end of the eighteenth century. In the twentieth century no less than 87 tribes have become extinct as the pace of development accelerates (Figure 7). From an estimated 2.5–5 million Indians who lived in Brazil in 1500, there are only some 150,000 left today. Now many Indians work as low-paid labourers in the white settlements. Once they have left their tribal areas many Indians find it difficult to adapt to modern ways. They become depressed, often turning to drink and crimes like prostitution.

▼ Fig 7
The impact of white civilisation on Brazilian Indians.

Western diseases — Loss of tribal land — Alcohol — Road construction — Slavery — **Indian population** — Plantations — Cattle ranches — Revengeful killing — Mining and forestry

1 a Which population group in Brazil has declined in numbers?

b When did this decline start?

c Give THREE reasons for this decline in population.

2 Look at the following statements and say whether you consider each one to be TRUE or FALSE. In each case explain your answer.

a The Indian culture is the oldest in Brazil.

b White settlers have helped improve the Indian way of life.

c Brazilian Indians are not affected by modern development.

32

# ECONOMIC ACTIVITIES

# 9. Booms and slumps

All too often Brazilians find headlines like these on the front pages of their newspapers. But bad years and good years are not new in Brazil. Until quite recently the Brazilian economy was heavily dependent on the export of primary products. These commodities came from the forests, mines and plantations which had been developed and exploited by the early Portuguese colonists. Indeed, since its discovery in 1500, Brazil has been through a series of **economic booms and slumps** (Figure 1). The start of each 'cycle' was marked by the discovery and exploitation of a valuable commodity which was exported to Europe and other overseas markets. The products were either precious minerals like gold, or commodities which could not be grown in Europe, like coffee. The Portuguese colonists exported these commodities which earned large revenues for Brazil. However, when the raw materials ran out or when **foreign competition** forced prices down, the boom ended. It was usually followed by a slump. Economic recovery occurred when a new export commodity was found.

Refer to the headlines and Figure 1.
**1 a** Which headlines bring (i) good news and (ii) bad news to Brazilian readers?

▼ Fig 1
Brazil's economic booms and slumps.

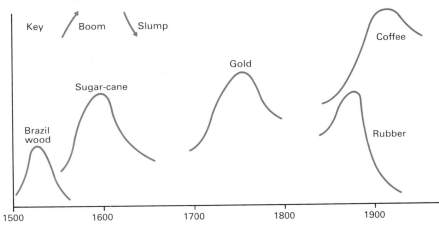

Key   ↗ Boom   ↘ Slump

Brazil wood · Sugar-cane · Gold · Coffee · Rubber

1500    1600    1700    1800    1900

▼ Fig 2
Three main types of economic activity.

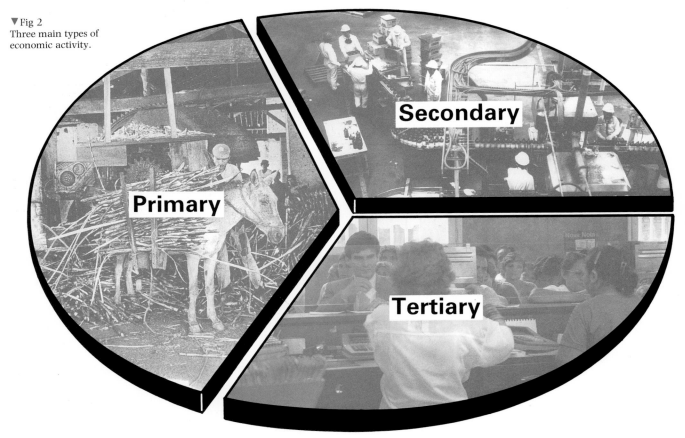

Primary

Secondary

Tertiary

**b** What are the two main features of an economic cycle?

**c** Name FOUR commodities that have followed economic cycles in Brazil.

**d** In which years (approximately) did each of these commodities reach the peak of their production?

**2** Why do you think European countries were an important market for Brazilian commodities?

**3 a** Refer to Figure 2. Name the three major types of economic activity.

**b** Which of these activities is represented by: (i) coffee and rubber production; (ii) gold mining; (iii) forestry?

## Four case studies: Economic cycles

**Brazil wood.** This special kind of wood was the first major export from Brazil. It was collected in the rainforests by Indians and traded to European settlers. Not only did this wood give its name to the country but it provided a valuable textile dye much in demand in sixteenth century Europe. As an economic activity, the collecting and processing of brazil wood was small-scale and localised. It required small amounts of labour and easy access to ports.

**Sugar-cane.** The establishment of sugar-cane production by the Portuguese had a much greater impact on Brazilian development. Huge farms called **plantations** were used to grow nothing but sugar in north-east Brazil. Sugar cultivation is back-breaking work requiring many labourers, but the North-east was thinly populated. The problem of this shortage of labour was resolved by importing slaves from Africa. The slave plantations marked the first

major stage in the modern economic development of Brazil. But as other regions, especially the West Indies, started to grow sugar, the world market price fell and the Brazilian economy slumped. The effect of this economic decline or **recession** was felt most severely in the North-east. Today, this region more than any other in Brazil suffers from serious economic problems and unemployment. These problems may be traced back to the decline of the sugar industry.

**Gold.** In the eighteenth century the focus of Brazilian development shifted inland to the gold and diamond mines in the state of Minas Gerais. But the **mining boom** was short-lived. However, it led to the start of an industry which later flourished with the discovery of new deposits and minerals like iron ore and bauxite.

**Rubber.** The gold rush was followed by the **rubber boom** which attracted many people to the Amazon region.

The rubber tree, *hevea brasiliensis*, is a native of the Amazon rainforest, but it does not grow in large stands as on a plantation. Consequently, exploitation of rubber was slow and expensive. When the British and other European powers set up rubber plantations in Malaya and other parts of South-east Asia, the collapse of Brazil's rubber trade was imminent. After 1912, production slumped rapidly. Rubber output today is small and there is little evidence of the rubber boom apart from cities like Manaus, which was largely built using 'rubber money', and Belem, which had become the most modern city in Brazil by the end of the nineteenth century. The great houses of the rubber barons and the famous Opera House in Manaus are relics of the prosperity brought to Brazil by the rubber boom.

▼ Fig 3
How coffee production helps the Brazilian economy.

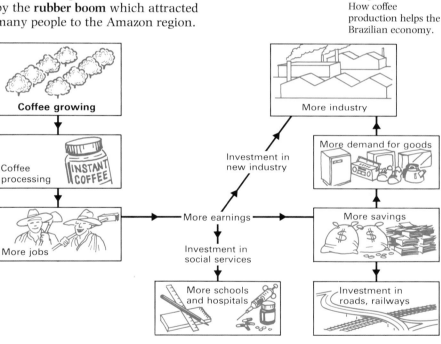

▼ Fig 4
Brazil's commodity exports in 1901 and 1982.

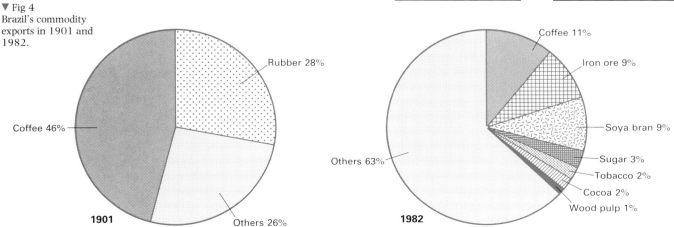

35

## The multiplier effect

The effect of the **coffee boom** was much more lasting than earlier economic cycles. The introduction of coffee in south-east Brazil had a multiplier effect (Figure 3). It lead to coffee processing industries, the development of roads and railways, and service industries such as banking. The city of São Paulo, which is located in the coffee region, owed its early prosperity and expansion to coffee production.

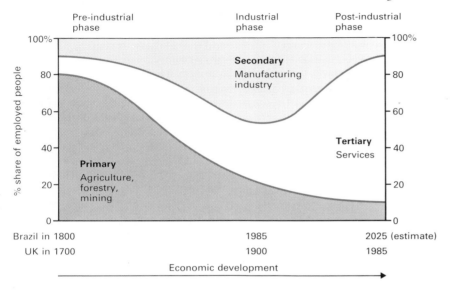

▼ Fig 5
A model of economic change.

1 Which two commodity booms had the least impact on the present economic development of Brazil?
2 a Name THREE factors that caused commodity slumps in Brazil.
  b Explain the effect of each factor you have listed.
3 Using the information in Figure 3, explain why coffee production had a major influence on the economic development of Brazil.
4 Study Figure 4 carefully.
  a Draw up two lists to show the commodities exported from Brazil in (i) 1982 and (ii) 1901.
  b Describe THREE changes that you can see from these lists.
5 Refer to Figure 5.
  a What stage of economic development had Brazil reached in (i) 1800; (ii) 1985?
  b Which sector of the economy do you think will expand most in the next phase of Brazil's economic development?
  c What kind of products do you think are represented by the groups labelled 'others' in Figure 4? Give reasons for your answers.

# 10. Farming patterns

## Farms large and small

In common with many less developed countries, Brazil has both large **commercial farms** and small **subsistence farms**. The main farming systems include the large estates or *latifundio* and peasant smallholdings, known as *minifundio*. Each farming system consists of two main elements. The farmer or landowner puts what are called farm **inputs** into the farm in order to grow crops or keep livestock. The products are known as farm **outputs**. It is the outputs of the farm that provide the landowner or farmer with an income or subsistence, that is, supplies of food for his family.

**1** Refer to Figures 1 and 2.
  **a** Match the photographs (Figures 1a and 1b) with the correct map (Figures 2a and 2b).
  **b** Name FOUR pieces of evidence that enabled you to match the photographs and maps.
**2** Study the farming system chart in Table 1.
  **a** Which system provides the farmer with (i) food for his family; (ii) crops for sale; (iii) the highest output *per capita* (per person); (iv) a secure livelihood; (v) the opportunity to use modern technology?
  **b** Explain why the minifundio system offers few prospects for the farmer in contrast to the latifundio system.
**3** Why do you think the latifundio is a more profitable farming system than the minifundio?

*Table 1    Brazil's main farming systems*

| Inputs/outputs | Minifundia | Latifundia |
|---|---|---|
| Capital | Small amount | Large amount |
| Crops | Food crops only | Cash crops for sale |
| Livestock | goats, hens, pigs | Beef cattle, sheep |
| Land (area) | Small (under 200 ha) | large (over 200 ha) |
| Security of tenure | generally poor | good |
| Labour | manual labour needed | little manual labour |
| Technology | simple tools | modern machinery |
| Output per person | low | high |

◄ Fig 1a
A sugar plantation in north-east Brazil.

► Fig 1b
A smallholding in north-east Brazil.

▼ Fig 2
The layout of two farms in Brazil.

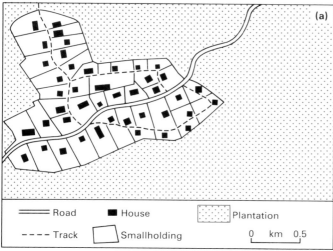

(a)

Road — House ■ — Plantation
Track - - - - Smallholding
0    km    0.5

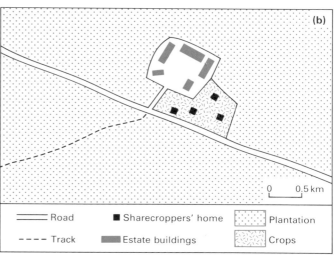

(b)

0    0.5 km

Road — Sharecroppers' home ■ — Plantation
Track - - - - Estate buildings — Crops

37

## Case study: Farming patterns in the Paracatu district

Paracatu lies in the north west of Minas Gerais, on the main road between Belo Horizonte and Brasilia. It is a plateau region dissected by the São Francisco River. With the exception of land on the valley floor, soils are poor. Even in this small district, which has a population of around 50,000, there are many different types of farming, as you can see from Table 2.

1 Study Table 2 carefully.
   a Which farms are run by (i) managers with absentee owners; (ii) owners with hired labour; (iii) owners and their families?
   b What are the main differences between the modern and traditional farms?
   c Which of the farms would you classify as (i) latifundio and (ii) minifundio?

2 With specific reference to Paracatu, state whether the following statements are true or false.
   a There is a wide range of farming methods in the district.
   b There are good educational opportunities for the children on all the farms.
   c With modern technology it is profitable to farm the poor soil of the plateau area.
   d The main road has helped all farmers to market their produce in nearby urban markets.
   e There are good opportunities for improving the methods of farming on the small subsistence farms.

## Changing patterns of farming

Many changes have occurred in Brazilian agriculture. The most significant trends are **mechanisation** and **crop diversification** (a wider variety of crops). The government has helped farmers by providing loans, or **rural credit**. In spite of this help, only the wealthier farmers can afford to buy tractors and other forms of mechanisation. Consequently, these are mainly used on the latifundio. The increased use of machinery on farms has raised the level of unemployment in rural areas.

Rural credit has also helped farmers buy chemical fertilizers and pesticides which have led to improved crop yields. More than two-thirds of Brazil's rural credit goes to farms in south and south-eastern Brazil. Most of this money goes towards increased production of coffee, sugar, rice, maize, soya and wheat. The trend is towards crop diversification, cattle ranching and **agribusinesses** or farm industries. These developments are helping to reduce Brazil's dependence

*Table 2   Six farms in the Paracatu district*

|  | FARM 1 Modern forestry and crops farm | FARM 2 Modern livestock farm | FARM 3 Modern arable farm | FARM 4 Traditional livestock farm | FARM 5 Traditional medium subsistence farm with surplus for sale | FARM 6 Traditional small subsistence farm |
|---|---|---|---|---|---|---|
| *Size in hectares* | 17,000 | 900 | 300 | 2,250 | 180 | 35 |
| *Land type* | Plateau | Plateau | Plateau | Plateau | Low hill slopes | Alluvial valley soil |
| *People on the property* | Manager and family, 260 labourers in 110 houses | Owner and 7 labourers | Husband, wife 3 children 1 labourer | Seven families sharing | Husband, wife 4 children, 1 labourer, labourer, wife | Husband, wife, 6 children under age 9 |
| *Home of owner* | Belo Horizonte | Belo Horizonte | Local | Local | Local | Local |
| *Technology* | 200 hectares irrigated, with fertiliser and high-yield seed | Tractor, truck and large use of fertiliser | Owns tractor, hires combine-harvester. Uses fertiliser and high-yield seed | Small mini-tractor. Mainly hand cultivation. No fertiliser | Small truck. Mainly hand cultivation | Hand cultivation. Water carried in tins from river |
| *Crops and cattle* | Planted timber including eucalypts, hay, rice, wheat, garlic | 1,000 cattle (300 sold a year). A few dairy cattle | Soya beans, rice | 300 cattle. Rice, maize, beans, cassava | 100 cattle, mainly beef. Rice, maize, beans, cassava | Mainly maize. Some rice, beans, cassava, chickens |
| *Market* | Charcoal for iron smelting in Belo Horizonte. Crops to Brasilia and Belo Horizonte | Cattle to Belo Horizonte market. Milk to co-operative in Paracatu | Soya beans and rice sold in a distant town | Paracatu | Milk and some cheese in Paracatu | Nothing to sell |
| *Other information* | Labourers well provided for: housing, schools and minimum wage | Pays minimum wage | Pays minimum wage; housing and cheap food for labourer | Children have grown up and moved to jobs in town | Pays minimum wage. Sells produce in own small shop in Paracatu | Barely enough to live on. Two oldest children kept from school to work on farm. Wife takes in washing |

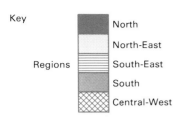

**Key**

**Regions**
- North
- North-East
- South-East
- South
- Central-West

**1. Share of all Brazilian farmland**

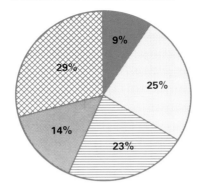

9%
25%
29%
14%
23%

**2. % of farmland cultivated**

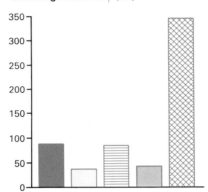

30%
20%
10%
0

**3. Number of tractors per cultivated hectare**

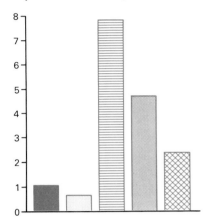

8
7
6
5
4
3
2
1
0

**4. Average farm size (ha)**

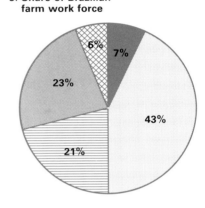

350
300
250
200
150
100
50
0

**5. Share of Brazilian farm work force**

6%
7%
23%
43%
21%

▲ Fig 3
Regional patterns in Brazilian agriculture.

on a small range of farm products (Table 3). But Brazil is no longer a predominantly agricultural country. In 1980 the agricultural sector of the economy accounted for 36 per cent of the work force and only 10 per cent of the Gross Domestic Product (GDP).

Study Table 3.

1 What evidence is there of crop diversification in Brazil between 1965 and 1975?

2 a Rank the crops according to (i) value and (ii) area.
  b What does this information tell you about the relative importance of these crops in Brazil? (You will need to explain which are the most and which the least important to the economy).
  c Name the three crops which yield the highest amount of money per hectare.

3 a Make two lists using the headings Food crops and Commercial cash crops. Work out the total cultivated area in hectares for these two categories.
  b Place yourself in the following roles, and decide whether you would give most support to food crops or commercial cash crops:
  (i) Government economic adviser; (ii) Peasant farmer; (iii) Oxfam Field Officer. Explain as fully as possible the reasons for each answer.

4 Study the graphs in Figure 3.
  a Give the names of the regions of Brazil which: (i) are the most and (ii) least modernised; (iii) have the largest and (iv) smallest average-sized farms; (v) have the most and (vi) least farm workers.

  b In which region would you expect to find the following farming conditions: (i) small, labour-intensive farms; (ii) very large ranches with only a small amount of cultivated land; (iii) small, highly mechanised farms with a high proportion of land under cultivation.

5 Using material from this section, try to justify the statement that the South and South-east are the most developed farming regions in Brazil.

Table 3   Changing crop patterns

| Major crops | Type | Value[1] | Production[2] | | Area[3] |
|---|---|---|---|---|---|
| | | 1973 | 1965 | 1975 | 1973 |
| Soya | Cash | 5,565 | 523 | 9,893 | 5,825 |
| Maize | Food | 5,123 | 12,112 | 16,335 | 10,855 |
| Rice | Food | 4,410 | 7,520 | 7,782 | 5,306 |
| Beans | Cash | 4,317 | 2,290 | 2,283 | 4,146 |
| Coffee | Cash | 3,988 | 3,664 | 2,545 | 2,217 |
| Manioc | Food | 3,465 | 24,993 | 26,118 | 2,042 |
| Sugar | Cash | 3,177 | 75,853 | 91,525 | 1,969 |
| Cotton | Cash | 3,888 | 1,986 | 1,748 | 3,877 |
| Wheat | Food | 1,495 | 585 | 1,788 | 2,932 |
| Oranges | Cash | 1,296 | 11,428 | 31,566 | 403 |
| Cocoa | Cash | 1,005 | 161 | 282 | 451 |
| Bananas | Cash | 937 | 349 | 364 | 314 |

[1] Value in millions of Cruzeiran dollars
[2] Production in '000 tonnes
[3] Area in '000 hectares

39

# 11. The land problem

## Who owns the land?

Nothing divides the people of rural Brazil more than the uneven distribution of land for farming. **Land ownership** is a major issue in Brazilian agriculture (Figures 1 and 2). Paracatu, in the north-west of Minas Gerais, is one district where much of the land is owned by a few families. Look at Table 1.

1 From the information in Table 1 draw two pie graphs to show the distribution of (i) population and (ii) land between the four main social groups in Paracatu.
2 Why do you think there is such a large proportion of landless people in Paracatu?
3 Which social group is most likely to migrate to cities? Give reasons for your choice.

*Table 1   Distribution of population and land in Paracatu*

| Social Group | Percentage of total population | Percentage of total land area |
|---|---|---|
| Large-scale farms | 4 | 72 |
| Medium-sized farms | 9 | 22 |
| Small farms | 23 | 6 |
| Landless people | 64 | — |

▶ Fig 1
A small part of one coffee plantation – and a major problem in Brazil.

▲ Fig 2
A landless peasant and family in north-east Brazil.

## Land is power

### HIRED GUNMEN GRAB SMALLHOLDING

Brazil's small farms are no longer safe, judging by recent reports. Using force when necessary, some big estate-owners are taking the law into their own hands. They hire gangs to push out the small farmers and then take over their land for profitable cash crops like sugar and soya.
Salvador, 18th May 1987.

Big landowners in Brazil are both rich and powerful. They have resisted attempts to introduce **land reform**, that is, the redistribution of land from large landowners to smallholders and landless peasants. The unequal pattern of land ownership that helped create the minifundio and latifundio systems was inherited from the colonial settlers. The new civilian government that came to power in 1985 supports land reform but it has been unable to change the position of the big landowners.

## Case study: São Francisco

'For four centuries now, the sugar fields between Salvador and São Francisco have bloomed. It all began under the third Governor-General, Mem de Sa, who governed Brazil from 1557 to 1574, after conquering this part of the country from the Indians and distributing it in fiefs (areas of control) to his lieutenants. Mem de Sa cultivated sugar-cane, and exported the "white gold" to the rapidly-growing European market ... The Indians' forced labour did not suffice to cultivate more than a fraction of his immense fief. So, in the seventeenth century, negro slaves began to be imported in great numbers. By inheritance and sales the land was divided up into a number of plantations ... a world where there were only lords and slaves ... This system has remained remarkably intact down the centuries.... In 1960 it was revealed that 83% of the population owned no land at all. Altogether 90% of those who were working in agriculture owned only 1.7% of the land.'

(Adapted from *Land and Power in South America*, Sven Lindqvist.)

1 How did land ownership in Brazil change after the arrival of European colonists?
2 What was the attitude of early colonists towards the Indians?
3 Why do you think land ownership is an issue in São Francisco today?
4 Land distribution is very uneven in north-east Brazil.
   a Using the data in Table 2, work out:
      (i) the percentage of farms that are over 200 hectares in size;
      (ii) the percentage of farms that are less than 50 hectares in size;
      (iii) the percentage of land owned by large (over 100 ha) farms;
      (iv) the percentage of land owned by small (less than 50 ha) farms.
   b Write a brief report to the Brazilian Ministry of Agriculture explaining the land problem in north-east Brazil. Use figures from Table 2 to back up your report.

## The Roca system

Long before the arrival of Europeans, the Indians practised **shifting cultivation** – sometimes called 'slash and burn' farming – using simple tools and traditional techniques (Figure 3). Once the site is chosen, the trees and undergrowth are cut down and burned. Tree stumps are left in, helping to prevent soil erosion. The clearing or **roca** is sown with a wide variety of subsistence crops including manioc which is the staple food of the Indians (Figure 4). As soil fertility declines rapidly once the protective forest cover has been removed, the site is evacuated after two or three years in favour of a new roca.

## *Pros and cons of the roca system*

Where the population density is sparse, the roca system is well-adapted to the tropical rainforest environment. Some experts believe it is the ideal farming method for Amazonia. However, in the North-east the system has led to widespread **deforestation**. In this region the pressure of population was greater. Consequently, the fallow time between periods of cultivation became too short for soils to regain their fertility. Rapid soil erosion generally followed, making the land useless for any further cultivation.

There is also the problem of **land tenure**. White settlers obtained titles or deeds for their land, giving them legal rights as farmers and security of tenure – they could not be evicted. But no such rights existed for the Indians practising shifting cultivation. Their traditional rights to land, based upon tribal custom, are not recognised by the Brazilian officials.

1 Briefly explain why the roca system is well-suited to the tropical rainforest environment.
2 Describe FOUR pieces of evidence in Figures 3 and 4 which suggest this is an area of roca cultivation.
3 Put yourself in the position of (i) a government official and (ii) an Indian roca farmer.
   a State your attitude towards the roca system of farming;
   b Explain why you think it should be given a proper legal status.

*Table 2 Unequal land ownership in north-east Brazil*

| Farm size in hectares[1] | Percentage of farms | Percentage of land |
| --- | --- | --- |
| 0–9 | 32.0 | 1.4 |
| 10–49 | 35.1 | 9.1 |
| 50–99 | 12.5 | 8.7 |
| 100–199 | 9.8 | 13.5 |
| 200–499 | 6.4 | 18.7 |
| 500 and over | 4.2 | 48.6 |

[1] One hectare (ha) is 2.47 acres

◄Figs 3 and 4 Clearing land for roca farming in the North-east; Bananas and manioc on a roca in Rondônia.

# 12. Plantations and ranches

## The plantation economy

One thing that is remarkable about Brazilian development is the extent to which it has been based on two everyday commodities. Coffee and sugar were the life-blood of the Brazilian economy. But the conditions that favoured sugar and coffee growing in Brazil are found in other tropical countries, and European powers like Britain and Spain turned to their colonies for tropical produce. The result was increased **competition** from these producers. Brazil is still a major producer of these commodities but its share of the **world markets** has declined steadily.

1 **a** From the data in Table 1 work out the Brazilian share of world sugar-cane and coffee production. Use this formula to do your calculations:

$$\frac{\text{Brazilian production}}{\text{World Production}} \times \frac{100}{1}$$

= % of world production

**b** Name Brazil's three main competitors in the production of (i) sugar-cane and (ii) coffee.

*Table 1   Leading sugar and coffee producers, 1984*

| World rank | Sugar | | Coffee | |
| | Country | Production* | Country | Production* |
| --- | --- | --- | --- | --- |
| 1 | Brazil | 241,518 | Brazil | 1,353 |
| 2 | India | 177,020 | Colombia | 780 |
| 3 | Cuba | 75,000 | Indonesia | 329 |
| 4 | China | 46,191 | Mexico | 262 |
| 5 | Mexico | 36,000 | Ethiopia | 240 |
| 6 | Pakistan | 34,287 | Uganda | 204 |
| 7 | Australia | 25,600 | El Salvador | 166 |
| 8 | USA | 25,427 | Philippines | 145 |
| 9 | Colombia | 24,000 | Guatemala | 140 |
| 10 | Indonesia | 23,726 | Cameroon | 127 |
| | WORLD | 935,769 | WORLD | 5,210 |

\* Production in '000 tonnes

**c** Work out their total share of world sugar and coffee production.
2 Refer to the map (Figure 1) which shows the distribution of major sugar and coffee growing areas in the nineteenth century, and to this list of leading producer states in the 1980s:
**Sugar**: São Paulo, Alagoas, Rio de Janeiro, Minas Gerais and Paraiba.
**Coffee**: Minas Gerais, São Paulo, Paraná, Espirito Santo, Bahia and Santa Catarina.
Describe how the distribution of sugar and coffee growing areas has changed since the nineteenth century.

## Case study 1: Coffee production

Brazil is the world's leading producer of coffee (Figure 2). What started as a garden crop in Rio de Janeiro in 1727 has spread to large plantations or **fazendas** in many parts of south-east Brazil, and sometimes on to land that is not ideally suited to the coffee plant. The coffee plant cannot withstand frost or strong winds and is easily damaged by pests like the coffee borer and a disease called leaf rust. Over the years, Brazilian production has fluctuated considerably (Figure 3). Now the Brazilians are developing new coffee technology to help combat hazards and to provide a more reliable supply of high-quality beans. Brazilian coffee growers no longer rely on traditional methods of cultivation.

## Traditional method of coffee cultivation

Reclaim land → clear undergrowth and large trees → burn all scrub in dry season → plant coffee beans directly in soil → cover young plants with wooden slats to protect from direct sunlight → coffee beans ready for harvesting after four years.

◄Fig 1
Coffee and sugar growing areas in the nineteenth century.

# 15. The Brazilian miracle

## The sleeping giant

'Like a sleeping giant, Brazil is awakening to a period of industrial expansion and development almost unparalleled among the countries of the Third World.'

That was how *The Times* described Brazil in 1973. Few countries have developed as rapidly as Brazil has done over the past twenty-five years. Brazil had the potential for rapid economic growth much earlier on but the conditions were not right. It possessed abundant natural resources and a large supply of labour. What Brazil needed was capital to exploit these resources and to invest in industry. As a relatively poor country, Brazil had to look overseas for help. A new, more stable government took control in 1964. It set out to attract foreign investment in order to transform Brazil into a modern industrial country as quickly as possible.

## Economic take-off

The economist Walt Rostow believed that economic development could be compared to an aeroplane taking off. He devised a model which showed

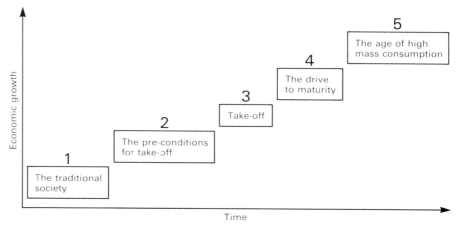

▲Fig 1
Rostow's stages of economic growth.

five stages of economic development (Figure 1). He claimed that all countries would eventually go through these stages. The idea behind this model came from the way industrialized countries like Britain had developed. Brazilian economic development has followed the **Rostow model** fairly closely but it has not yet reached Stage 5 (Figure 2).

1 a How many stages are there in Rostow's economic growth model?
  b What is meant by *pre-conditions for take-off*?
  c Describe the pre-conditions for take-off in Brazil.

d What were the main economic results of take-off in Brazil?
e What evidence is there to support the view that Brazil has not reached Stage 5 of the Rostow Model?

2 Using the information in Table 1
  a list the five main types of business (e.g. cars) according to turnover (sales);
  b work out the number of businesses owned by: (i) Brazil; (ii) The USA; (iii) West Germany (FRG); (iv) The UK; (v) The Netherlands; (vi) Other foreign countries.

3 How do you think foreign companies have contributed towards the Brazilian 'economic miracle'?

▼Fig 2
The stages of Brazilian economic development.

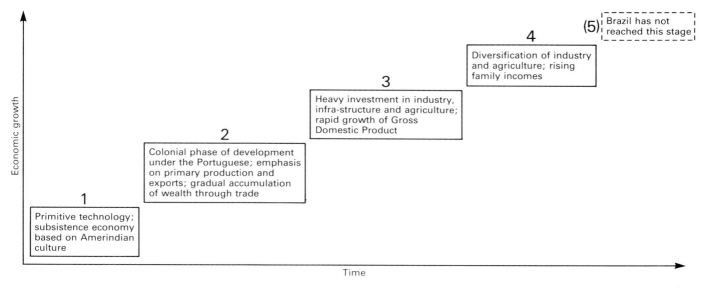

Table 1   Major companies in Brazil, 1987

| Rank | Company | Type of Business | Sales/Turnover[1] | Ownership |
|------|---------|------------------|-------------------|-----------|
| 1 | Petrobras | Petroleum | 9,465 | Brazil |
| 2 | Petrobras Distribuidora | Petroleum | 2,426 | Brazil |
| 3 | Pao de Acucar | Supermarkets | 1,821 | Brazil |
| 4 | Shell | Petroleum | 1,579 | UK/N'lands |
| 5 | Telebras | Telecommunications | 1,521 | Brazil |
| 6 | Texaco Brazil | Petroleum | 1,300 | US |
| 7 | Volkswagen do Brasil | Cars | 1,201 | FRG |
| 8 | Esso Brasileira de Petroleo | Petroleum | 1,112 | US |
| 9 | Souza Cruz Ind e Comercio | Beverages, tobacco | 1,002 | UK |
| 10 | Mendes Junior | Heavy construction | 866 | Brazil |
| 11 | Copersucar | Sugar, alcohol | 855 | Brazil |
| 12 | General Motors do Brasil | Cars | 849 | US |
| 13 | Vale do Rio Doce | Iron mining | 826 | Brazil |
| 14 | Embratel | Telecommunications | 795 | Brazil |
| 15 | Atlantic de Petroleo | Petroleum | 767 | US |
| 16 | Usiminas | Steel | 729 | Brazil |
| 17 | Copene | Petrochemicals | 700 | Brazil |
| 18 | Siderurgica Nacional | Steel | 694 | Brazil |
| 19 | Electropaulo | Electricity | 679 | Brazil |
| 20 | Ford Brasil | Cars | 661 | US |
| 21 | Varig | Airline | 611 | Brazil |
| 22 | Petroleo Ipiranga | Petroleum | 610 | Brazil |
| 23 | Cosipa–Siderurgica Paulista | Steel | 559 | Brazil |
| 24 | CESP | Electricity | 539 | Brazil |
| 25 | Pirelli | Plastics, rubber | 539 | Italy |
| 26 | Mercedes-Benz do Brasil | Cars | 513 | FRG |
| 27 | Interbras–Petrobras Com Int | Commerce | 511 | Brazil |
| 28 | Fiat Automoveis | Cars | 504 | Italy |
| 29 | Rede Ferroviaria Federal | Railways | 438 | Brazil |
| 30 | Andrade Gutierrez | Heavy construction | 436 | Brazil |
| 31 | Rhodia | Chemicals | 425 | France |
| 32 | Nestlé | Food | 423 | Switzerland |
| 33 | Agricola de Cotia | Agribusiness | 399 | Brazil |
| 34 | Camargo Correa Industrial | Heavy construction | 399 | Brazil |
| 35 | Telesp | Telecommunications | 397 | Brazil |
| 36 | Furnas Centrais Eletricas | Power plant | 388 | Brazil |
| 37 | IBM | Computers | 373 | US |
| 38 | Sanbra | Vegetable oils | 363 | Argentina |
| 39 | Goodyear | Plastics, rubber | 354 | US |
| 40 | Gessy Lever | Detergents | 347 | UK/N'lands |
| 41 | Tubarao-CST | Steel | 332 | Brazil |
| 42 | Cutrale | Food | 322 | Brazil |
| 43 | CBA–Brasileira de Aluminio | Aluminium | 321 | Brazil |
| 44 | Norberto Odebrecht | Heavy construction | 315 | Brazil |
| 45 | Carrefour | Supermarkets | 306 | Brazil |
| 46 | Petroquimica Uniao | Petrochemicals | 303 | Brazil |
| 47 | Cemig | Power plant | 302 | Brazil |
| 48 | Philips do Brasil | Electronics | 295 | N'lands |
| 49 | Light | Electricity | 294 | Brazil |
| 50 | Paulista de Forca e Luz | Electricity supply | 290 | Brazil |

[1]$US million

## Winners and losers

Some of the results of the Brazilian 'miracle' are all too clear (Figures 3 and 4). As in any race against time there are winners and losers. The Brazilian 'miracle' was a success story for the government and big businesses. But for many of the people who helped build the new Brazil there has been very little progress. The growth of industry helped create wealth and new jobs in factories. But levels of pay are often extremely low, so low that most rural migrants cannot afford decent housing. The most they can hope for is a home-made shack in one of the **shanty towns**. So industrialization has led to rapid urban growth. In spite of the poverty in the shanty towns, the standard of living in Brazil's cities is much higher than in the rural areas. The region that attracted most industrial development was south-east Brazil. In fact, south-east Brazil is almost a country within a country because family incomes and job opportunities are so much better than in most other parts of Brazil. The employment figures in Table 2 show the spread of manufacturing industry and tertiary or service industries like banking, commerce and tourism. But how did ordinary people like the factory workers benefit? To answer that question, notice how the distribution of income changed between 1960 and 1980 (Figure 5). Each sector in these diagrams represents a fifth of the workforce. If Brazil's wealth was shared equally, then each sector would receive a fifth of the total income for the country. Yet the poorest group received only 2 per cent of the national income in 1980.

1 Draw bar graphs to show employment in 1950 and 1980, using the data given in Table 2. Draw separate graphs for each employment sector.
2 Describe the main trends or changes that have occurred in each employment sector between 1950 and 1980.
3 How do you account for (i) the growth of employment in manufacturing and (ii) the decline of employment in agriculture?
4 Explain why *The Times* described Brazil as a 'sleeping giant'.
5 Write captions to Figures 3 and 4 to illustrate the idea that there are winners and losers in Brazil today.
6 Describe THREE major ways in which industrialization has affected the development of Brazil.

Figs 3 and 4
Modern prosperity
and poverty in
Brazil.

Table 2    Changing patterns of employment in Brazil

| | Percentage of workforce | | | |
| Employment Sector | 1950 | 1960 | 1970 | 1980 |
| --- | --- | --- | --- | --- |
| Agriculture | 59.9 | 54.0 | 44.3 | 30.5 |
| Manufacturing | 14.2 | 13.2 | 18.4 | 24.9 |
| Commerce and Service Industries | 15.4 | 18.6 | 19.9 | 26.1 |
| Transport and Communication | 4.0 | 4.6 | 4.1 | 4.2 |
| Social services and Public administration | 6.5 | 9.6 | 13.3 | 14.3 |

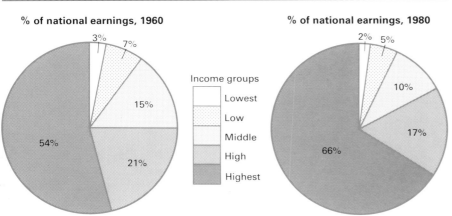

% of national earnings, 1960

3%  7%
15%
54%
21%

Income groups

Lowest
Low
Middle
High
Highest

% of national earnings, 1980

2%  5%
10%
17%
66%

◀ Fig 5 The division
of wealth in Brazil.

# 16. Industry in Brazil

## *Technology or people?*

Brazil is a rapidly industrializing country. Until recently it has relied heavily on a ready supply of cheap labour to work in its factories. Most of the traditional industries like clothes manufacture are **labour intensive**: they depend upon people rather than machines to do most of the work. In the backstreets of most cities in Brazil there are hundreds of small workshop industries. These workshops may have very simple equipment, but they produce utility or convenience goods that are inexpensive and affordable by most people. However, Brazil is turning to high technology industries that use machines and computers as a way of increasing the manufacturing output. These industries are **capital intensive**,

▲Fig 1a
Assembling television sets in a factory in São Paulo.

◄Fig 1b
Manufacturing chemicals in São Paulo.

▼ Fig 1c
Metal working in Recife.

requiring large sums of money to set up. In order to obtain this capital, the government encouraged **multinational companies** to set up in Brazil, as well as starting up state-owned businesses.

1 a Match each picture in Figure 1 with the appropriate description:
   (i) this factory uses expensive technology and has a small workforce;
   (ii) this is a labour-intensive factory depending upon a large workforce;
   (iii) this is a workshop that has a small, skilled workforce.
  b Using the information in Figure 1, describe three different kinds of manufacturing industry in Brazil.

Table 1 Setting up business in Brazil

| Company | Estimated employment | | Estimated annual exports ($USM) | |
|---|---|---|---|---|
| | (A) | (B) | (A) | (B) |
| Peach Computers Ltd | 500 | 1,000 | 1.5 | 3.0 |
| Sampson Trucks Ltd | 1,000 | 1,500 | 2.0 | 5.0 |
| Sunsquash drinks Pty | 750 | 2,500 | 0.75 | 2.5 |

(A) after two years of operation; (B) after 5 years of operation

2 In this simulation exercise you are asked to consider the advantages of setting up a new company in Brazil.

**Your role:** an economic adviser to the government.
**Your job:** to advise the government on suitable new industries.
**Your priorities:** making a profit and creating jobs.

The companies that want to set up business in Brazil are shown in Table 1, together with information about estimated employment and export earnings.

a Rank the three industries in order of suitability. Explain how you arrived at your rankings.
b State how each industry would benefit Brazil in terms of (i) job creation and (ii) export earnings.

## Modern industries in Brazil

There are two industries that have played a particularly important part in Brazil's economic development: steel manufacture and motor vehicle manufacture. Both these industries have helped to reduce Brazil's dependence on imported goods. They are sometimes called **import substitution industries** because they save Brazil from buying steel and motor vehicles from overseas. The iron and steel industry also plays a valuable role in supporting other industries. It supplies all kinds of steel products to other manufacturing industries, such as shipbuilding. As Brazil is going for a road-based economy, the motor industry was started up to provide people and businesses with transport. As a result, there is a close link between steel production and motor vehicle manufacture. Brazil is a major world producer of both steel and motor vehicles (Table 2).

## Case study 1: The iron and steel industry

The location of the major steelworks in Brazil reflects the influence of several factors. Study Figure 2. The main locational advantage of south-east Brazil is the presence of huge deposits of high grade iron ore, as well as limestone and manganese which are the basic **raw materials** for making steel. These mineral resources

▼ Fig 2
The location of major integrated and semi-integrated steelworks.

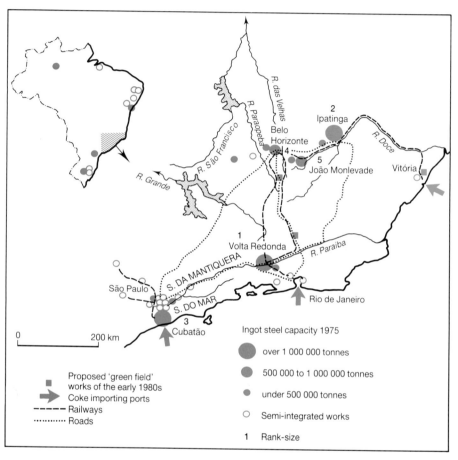

Table 2 Major steel and car producers in 1984

| Country | Steel (million tonnes) | Cars (thousands) |
|---|---|---|
| USSR | 153,996 | 1,296 |
| Japan | 105,588 | 7,073 |
| USA | 82,716 | 7,622 |
| China | 43,320 | n/a |
| W. Germany | 39,384 | 3,788 |
| Italy | 23,076 | 1,439 |
| France | 19,020 | 2,910 |
| Brazil | 18,384 | 536 |
| Poland | 16,536 | 280 |
| UK | 15,120 | 90 |
| Czechoslovakia | 14,832 | 180 |
| Canada | 14,700 | 1,033 |
| Spain | 13,572 | 1,174 |
| Belgium | 11,304 | 890[1] |
| World total | 653,000 | 30,000 |

[1] Car assembly only

◀ Fig 3
The Volta Redonda
Steelworks.

▼ Fig 4
The Fiat factory at
Belo Horizonte.

are all found close together in the
state of Minas Gerais. Brazil's steel
industry dates from 1925 when the
first factory was completed. Since
then over twenty steelworks, mainly
state-owned, have been built.

Volta Redonda has the largest
steelworks in Brazil and the whole of
South America. Built in 1947 by the
National Steel Company of Brazil,
Volta Redonda is an **integrated
steelworks** where all the steel-making
processes from pig-iron to finished
steel production are carried out on
one site (Figure 3). It produces steel
plates, sheets and coils, galvanised
plate, high-carbon steel, medium and
heavy steel parts, rails and track.
Only four other steelworks in Brazil
have the capacity to make more than
500,000 tonnes of steel a year.

## Case study 2: The motor industry

The first Brazilian car was a Model
'T' Ford which was assembled from
imported parts or components in São
Paulo in 1919. Today over a million
vehicles are made in Brazil each year.
The motor industry requires high-
level technology, a skilled workforce
and massive capital investment. It
also stimulates other industries
because of the wide variety of
components that make up a finished
vehicle. The government encouraged
multinational companies like Ford to
invest in Brazil in order to set up the
industry and obtain the latest
technology from Europe and North
America. The results of this policy
may be seen in Table 3.

Table 3  Vehicle production in Brazil, 1981

| Make | Origin | Type of vehicle | '000 units |
|---|---|---|---|
| Volkswagen | W. Germany | Cars and trucks | 304.6 |
| General Motors | USA | Cars, trucks and buses | 155.6 |
| Fiat | Italy | Cars and trucks | 133.2 |
| Ford | USA | Cars, trucks and buses | 126.8 |
| Mercedes-Benz | W. Germany | Trucks and buses | 49.0 |
| Toyota | Japan | Trucks | 4.0 |
| Saab-Scania | Norway | Trucks and buses | 3.5 |
| Volvo | Sweden | Trucks and buses | 1.6 |

Belo Horizonte is the home of the
huge Fiat factory which was opened
in 1978 (Figure 4). It produces over
130,000 cars a year and has a
workforce of over 10,000. Nearby
component factories employ
thousands more workers. But the
high technology used in vehicle
production means there are only jobs
for suitably skilled people (Figure 5).
It is for this reason that the motor
industry has not helped to solve the
major problem of unemployment in
Brazil's cities.

1 From Table 2 find out where Brazil
ranks in the world as a producer of
(i) steel and (ii) cars.

▲ Fig 5
Inside a car factory.

integrated steelworks. Make sure your diagram is clearly labelled. Refer to the text and Figure 3 for the information.

5 Study Figure 6 carefully, following the sequence of events along the motor vehicle production line.
   a Name EIGHT main areas of production in a motor vehicle factory.
   b At which stage on the production line was the photograph in Figure 5 taken?
   c Which parts of the vehicles are NOT made on the motor vehicle production line? Where are these parts of the vehicle made?

6 Describe THREE factors that would have been important in deciding the location of the Fiat car plant shown in Figure 4.

7 The motor industry has a **multiplier effect** because it leads to the growth of other industries. Make a list of at least FIVE examples and explain how they are connected with the manufacture of motor vehicles.

8 Why do you think Brazil's industrialization strategy has not solved the serious problem of unemployment?

3 Referring to Figure 2
   a Name ONE kind of raw material for steel making that is imported.
   b What do you notice about the location of the proposed 'green field' sites (outside traditional centres of industry) for new steelworks?

4 a Explain what is meant by the term 'integrated steelworks'.
   b Name ONE example of an integrated steelworks in Brazil.
   c Draw a flow diagram to show the main steel making processes in an

2 a Name THREE major steelworks in Brazil.
   b Give FOUR reasons why Brazil's steel industry is mainly located in the south-east region.

▼ Fig 6
A motor vehicle production line.

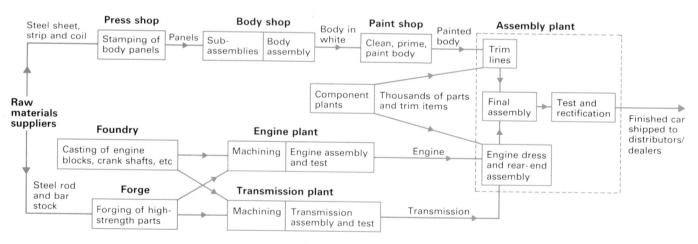

57

# 17. Energy for development

▲ Fig 1
Filling up with alcohol fuel.

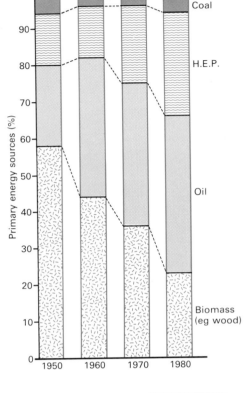

▶ Fig 2
The changing pattern of energy production in Brazil.

## Dependence on oil

Figure 1 shows a common sight in Brazil today. Why do Brazilian drivers not always use ordinary petrol? The fact is that Brazil has an **energy problem**. The rapid growth of industry and road transport means that Brazil requires huge amounts of oil. But Brazilian oilfields are small and production is limited so that nearly all oil supplies have to be imported. When Brazil started to industrialize rapidly in the 1960s, oil was the best energy option. It was relatively cheap and Brazil had few alternative sources of enery such as coal. However, in 1974 the major oil producing and exporting countries – **OPEC** – put up the price of a barrel of oil from $US3.45 to $8.70. The world oil crisis followed as prices continued to soar to $32 a barrel. This hit the Brazilian economy very hard because it had become dependent on imported oil.

You will need to study the information in the graphs and diagram (Figures 2, 3 and 4) before answering these questions.

1 a Name the FIVE main sources of energy in Brazil in 1980.
  b Work out the relative importance of each source of energy by calculating the percentage of the total energy production in the following years:
  (i) 1950; (ii) 1960; (iii) 1970 and (iv) 1980.

2 a Which source of energy has decreased in importance most since 1950?

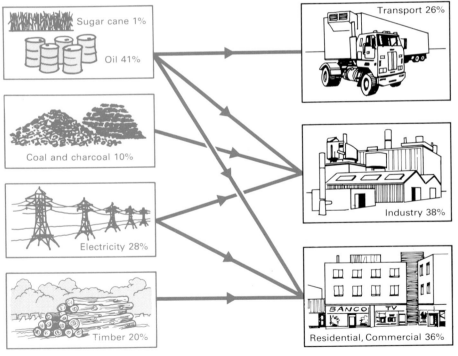

▲ Fig 3
Where the energy goes in Brazil.

b Which was the least important source of energy in 1980?
c Which sources of energy are (i) renewable and (ii) non-renewable? (See page 26)

3 Which TWO sources of energy do you predict will be most important in the

year 2000? Give reasons for your predictions.

4 In 1976 the most highly developed region of the South-east, including São Paulo and Rio de Janeiro, consumed three-quarters of Brazil's electricity. Using the information in Figure 3, explain why Brazil's consumption of energy is concentrated in this region.

5 Imagine you are a journalist reporting on Brazil's oil crisis. Write a short piece describing the problem that is represented in Figure 4.

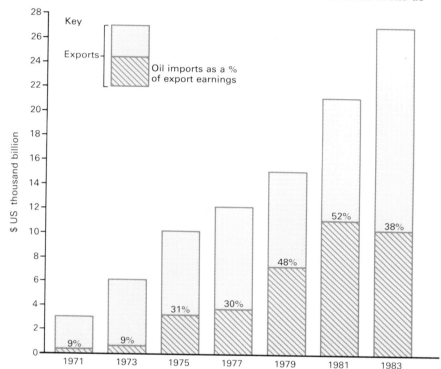

▲ Fig 4
The cost of oil imports as a percentage of export earnings.

## Energy strategies for the future

The oil crisis prompted the Brazilian government to look for ways of providing energy more cheaply. Also, it wanted to become less dependent on supplies of oil from abroad. So the government came up with four solutions, each of which is beginning to help reduce Brazil's dependence on imported oil.

1 The search for oil in Brazil is being stepped up.
2 Water power (HEP) is being exploited more fully.
3 Nuclear power is being developed using the energy of uranium.
4 The alcohol fuel programme is being expanded.

## Strategy 1

The Brazilian national oil company, PETROBRAS, has invested heavily in **oil exploration**. Several small oilfields have been discovered. In the North-east between Salvador and Maceio there are on- and off-shore wells, but they produce only a tenth of Britain's North Sea oil production. In 1974 oil was struck in the Campos Basin which lies between 80 and 120 kilometres off the coast of Rio de Janeiro. Ten years later over three hundred wells had been sunk. The search for oil continues, especially in the Amazon Basin, but it seems unlikely that Brazil will become self-sufficient in oil.

## Strategy 2

Only twenty-three per cent of Brazil's huge potential for **hydroelectric power** (HEP) has been tapped. The main reasons for the lack of HEP lie in the high cost of constructing dams and power stations and the fact that the best sites for dams lie far away from centres of population and industry. Several large projects are under construction, including the Itaipu Complex on the Paraná River. This complex is being built jointly by Brazil and Paraguay (Figure 5). It will be the largest HEP scheme in the world, generating six times as much electric power as the Aswan High Dam on the River Nile in Egypt. The scheme has created a huge lake, flooding villages, farmland and forests, displacing over 20,000 people. Not surprisingly, there is a strong **environmental lobby** from pressure groups that oppose big dam projects. A further twelve hydroelectric schemes are under construction, mainly in the Paraná and São Francisco river basins.

▼Fig 5
The Itaipu Dam on the River Paraná under construction.

## Strategy 3

Brazil is developing **nuclear energy** with the technical help of West Germany. Originally, eight nuclear power stations were planned but only one, located at Angra dos Reis near Rio de Janeiro, has been completed so far. The very high cost of nuclear energy as well as environmental and safety concerns have thrown doubts on the future of this option.

## Strategy 4

Why not drive your car on **alcohol fuel**? (Figure 6). The idea is not as strange as it may seem for Brazil has a flourishing ethyl alcohol (ethanol) industry. The ethanol is distilled from sugar-cane in what are called agro-distilleries. The technology for ethanol production is quite straightforward. The distilleries – there are already over three hundred – use Brazilian sugar-cane. As well as providing cheap fuel for motor vehicles, the Alcohol Programme has put new life into the sugar-cane

*It's all right, sir. It's only suffering from a hangover!*

▲ Fig 6

business in the poverty-stricken North-east. The area of land used for sugar-cane will need to be almost doubled in order to keep up with demand for ethanol. At the start of the programme the aim was to convert cars to take twenty per cent alcohol mixed with petrol. In 1975 the new target was to produce one hundred per cent alcohol-run cars. In response, companies like Fiat, VW, Ford and General Motors now make all-alcohol powered cars.

As a result of these energy strategies, Brazil's dependence on imported oil has fallen from 45% in 1975 to 30% in 1981. In spite of this reduction, oil still represents nearly half the value of all imported goods.

1 a What energy strategy did the Brazilian government adopt in (i) the 1960s and (ii) the 1980s?
  b Explain why the government changed its attitude towards its oil-based style of economic development.
2 Design a poster advertising the Alcohol Programme. The message should be clear and simple. Compare your poster with others in the class and discuss the different methods of persuading drivers to go for the alcohol option.

# PATTERNS OF DEVELOPMENT

# 18. The development puzzle

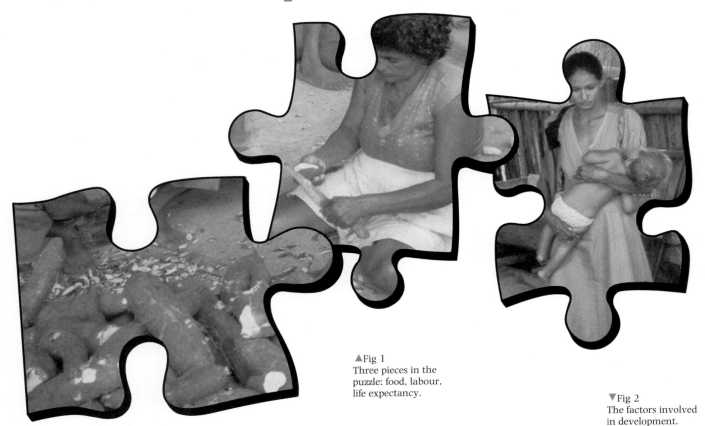

▲Fig 1
Three pieces in the puzzle: food, labour, life expectancy.

▼Fig 2
The factors involved in development.

## Less developed or more developed?

What impressions do you have of life in the **less developed countries**, sometimes called the Third World? In **more developed countries** like Britain, we are influenced by the pictures in the news. They generally convey a dismal picture of poverty, hunger and disease. But how correct is this popular stereotype of a less developed country? Would it apply to Brazil? To answer these questions we need to look carefully at what we mean by development and how we measure it. Development is rather like a jigsaw puzzle – made up of many pieces (Figure 1). This is because there are many factors involved in development, as you can see from Figure 2. As with a jigsaw puzzle, the whole picture can be seen only when all the pieces have been put together. Development is not just about **economic growth** or **social conditions** such as health. It concerns factors like our customs and beliefs, which are part of our culture, as well as the quality of our environment and technical matters like factory methods and medical skills.

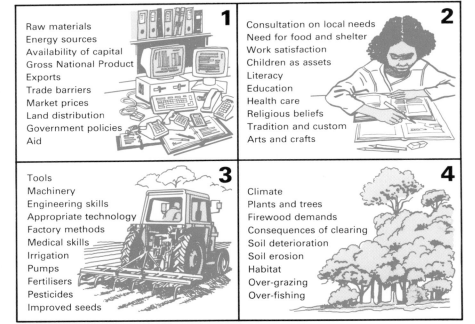

**1**
Raw materials
Energy sources
Availability of capital
Gross National Product
Exports
Trade barriers
Market prices
Land distribution
Government policies
Aid

**2**
Consultation on local needs
Need for food and shelter
Work satisfaction
Children as assets
Literacy
Education
Health care
Religious beliefs
Tradition and custom
Arts and crafts

**3**
Tools
Machinery
Engineering skills
Appropriate technology
Factory methods
Medical skills
Irrigation
Pumps
Fertilisers
Pesticides
Improved seeds

**4**
Climate
Plants and trees
Firewood demands
Consequences of clearing
Soil deterioration
Soil erosion
Habitat
Over-grazing
Over-fishing

**1 a** Figure 2 shows four groups of factors in development. They are numbered 1–4. Match each of these numbers with the following groups of factors: economic; social and cultural; technical; environmental.

**b** Write a sentence explaining each group, to show you understand what the different terms mean.

**2** Describe your impressions of less developed countries. Say how you formed these impressions (for example, from reading or watching television programmes), and whether you think they are likely to be accurate.

## Ladders of development

Using **development indicators** it is possible to measure Brazil's **level of development** and to compare it with other countries. Economic indicators like Gross National Product (GNP) per capita and manufacturing output tell us about the general level of wealth in a country. The social indicators tell us about the general standard of living, quality of welfare and education within the country as a whole. What these development indicators do not tell us is how the benefits of development are distributed amongst the population. Also, some aspects of development are not easy to measure, like human rights, people's happiness, customs and environmental quality.

Like many less developed countries, Brazil has made choices about the way it is developing. In Figure 3 the levels of development are represented by the rungs on a ladder. Through its policy of rapid industrialization, Brazil has climbed well up the ladders of wealth and economic production. Using these indicators alone it appears that Brazil is a relatively

developed country now. How, then, does Brazil's social development compare with its economic performance and with the social development of other countries? The data in Table 1 may be used to compare the social development of ten countries.

**1 a** Using the data in Table 1, draw THREE development ladders showing: (i) infant mortality; (ii) diet; (iii) adult literacy.
  **b** Refer to Figure 3 and Table 1. Select the countries which fit the following descriptions: (i) the least wealthy; (ii) the least favourable ratio of population to doctors; (iii) the least adequate diet; (iv) the lowest life expectancy; (v) the highest level of infant mortality.
  **c** Complete a table to show Brazil's rank for each indicator used in Figure 3 and Table 1. (Note that 1 is the highest rank and 10 is the lowest. For some indicators a high rank is given for low figures, as in the case of infant mortality).
  **d** What does this table tell you about the relative levels of social and economic development in Brazil?

**2 a** Which aspects of development are not easy to measure?
  **b** Why do you think these aspects of development are particularly important to individual people?
  **c** Suggest ways you might attempt to measure any one of them.

## The development gap

The gulf in wealth and living standards between more developed and less developed countries is usually called the **development gap**. As a rapidly developing country, Brazil has outstripped many less developed countries, having passed the stage of economic 'take off' in the 1960s (see page 51). It is far wealthier than the world's poorest countries, but prosperity and social development have not reached many people in Brazil. There is still much poverty. The 'trickle down' theory does not seem to have worked. Brazil's top-heavy style of

▼ Fig 3
Ladders of development.

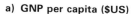

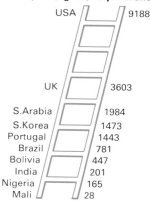

a) **GNP per capita ($US)**

| | |
|---|---|
| USA | 13 968 |
| S.Arabia | 12 094 |
| UK | 8460 |
| Portugal | 2370 |
| S.Korea | 1999 |
| Brazil | 1640 |
| Bolivia | 1054 |
| Nigeria | 800 |
| Mali | 297 |
| India | 270 |

b) **Value of exports per capita ($US)**

| | |
|---|---|
| S.Arabia | 7132 |
| UK | 1789 |
| USA | 847 |
| S.Korea | 452 |
| Portugal | 422 |
| Brazil | 189 |
| Bolivia | 151 |
| Nigeria | 126 |
| India | 13 |
| Mali | 12 |

c) **Energy consumption per capita (kg coal equivalent)**

| | |
|---|---|
| USA | 9188 |
| UK | 3603 |
| S.Arabia | 1984 |
| S.Korea | 1473 |
| Portugal | 1443 |
| Brazil | 781 |
| Bolivia | 447 |
| India | 201 |
| Nigeria | 165 |
| Mali | 28 |

d) **% labour force in agriculture**

| | |
|---|---|
| | 0% |
| UK | 2 |
| USA | 3 |
| Portugal | 24 |
| Brazil | 30 |
| S.Korea | 34 |
| Bolivia | 50 |
| S.Arabia | 61 |
| India | 69 |
| Nigeria | 70 |
| Mali | 73 |
| | 100% |

Table 1  Social indicators of development, 1985

| | Infant mortality[1] | Diet[2] | Population per doctor | Adult literacy[3] | Life expectancy[4] |
|---|---|---|---|---|---|
| Brazil | 77 | 2,562 | 1,700 | 76 | 63 |
| Bolivia | 131 | 1,974 | 1,850 | 63 | 50 |
| India | 123 | 2,021 | 3,630 | 36 | 52 |
| Nigeria | 109 | 2,185 | 12,000 | 34 | 50 |
| Portugal | 71 | 3,076 | 700 | 65 | 71 |
| Saudi Arabia | 114 | 2,624 | 1,700 | 16 | 54 |
| South Korea | 34 | 2,785 | 1,980 | 93 | 65 |
| Mali | 154 | 2,117 | 25,560 | 9 | 43 |
| UK | 12 | 3,336 | 750 | 99 | 73 |
| USA | 13 | 3,576 | 750 | 99 | 72 |

[1] per 1000 population;   [2] daily calorie supply;   [3] percentage of population;   [4] average age.

development has produced great contrasts within the country. For example, Brazil has a high technology space programme capable of putting satellites into orbit by 1989. In the same year there will be over 40 million Brazilians who will not have adequate food, housing and health care, and many Brazilian Indians who will lose their homes and livelihood.

**1 a** What is another name given to the less developed countries?
  **b** What does the expression 'development gap' mean?

2 Imagine you are sending some pictures showing contrasting scenes in Brazil to a friend in Britain (Figure 4). Write a short letter to accompany the pictures saying what each one tells you about the development gap in Brazil.

3 Using Brazil as your example, explain why it is difficult to draw a dividing line between areas of the world that are more developed and less developed.

▶ Fig 4a
Spending or collecting? A street scene in São Paulo.

◀ Fig 4b
These migrants have just arrived in Amazonia to start a new life.

▶ Fig 4c
Children playing outside in a village.

◀ Fig 4d
An Indian home and possessions.

# 19. The urban scene

▲ Fig 1a
Rio de Janeiro.
Copacabana beach
and exclusive
apartments.

► Fig 1b
Another view of Rio
de Janeiro – in a
favela.

## The urban explosion

What do you think the buildings in Figure 1 have in common? Perhaps not very much when you consider the vast contrast in living standards and wealth. But these scenes show two sides of city growth in Brazil. The urban explosion in Brazil has led to modern high-rise buildings in city centres and sprawling shanty towns, or **favelas** as they are known locally. Brazil is becoming rapidly urbanized. In most developing countries less than three out of every ten people live in towns and cities. This was true of Brazil thirty years ago. Today seven out of every ten Brazilians live in urban areas, and the proportion of urban dwellers is rising steadily. Brazil is now an **urban society**, with urban occupations, living conditions and values (Table 1).

The transformation from a rural to an urban society has resulted in the massive growth of Brazil's major cities, such as Rio de Janeiro and São Paulo (Figure 2). These large cities act like magnets on the countryside, drawing people away from their villages and rural occupations (Figure 3). This process is called **rural migration**. It is one of the main reasons for the urban explosion in Brazil. Other factors like immigration and industrialization have also led to rapid urbanization.

1 What does Figure 1 reveal about Rio de Janeiro?
2 Referring to Figure 2:
   a Name (i) the THREE largest cities in Brazil; (ii) the fastest-growing city in Brazil.
   b Write down the names of Brazil's FIVE major cities in order of size in (i) 1900; (ii) 1940 and (iii) 1980.
   c During which of these periods did Brazil's urban explosion take place? (i) 1872 to 1890; (ii) 1900 to 1920; (iii) 1940 to 1950; (iv) 1950 onwards.
   d Give THREE reasons for Brazil's urban explosion.
3 a What proportion of Brazil's population live in cities?
   b Describe THREE ways in which

Table 1   Contrasts between urban and rural societies

|  | Urban | Rural |
|---|---|---|
| Occupations | office/factory jobs, e.g. banking, business, manufacturing. | home/farm jobs, e.g. farming, weaving, pottery. |
| Living conditions | Modern flats/houses. Many amenities, e.g. electricity; clean water, main drains. | Simple houses/huts. Few amenities, e.g. water from wells; open latrines; no electricity. |
| Values | Modern, consumer society; leisure-oriented; highly mobile. | Traditional subsistence society; work-oriented; little mobility. |

Note: living conditions in many favelas are similar to those in rural areas

65

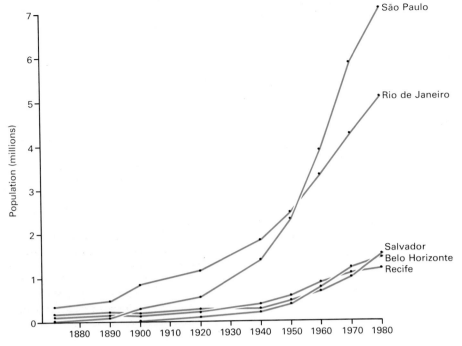

São Paulo and Rio de Janeiro stand out because they are much larger than any other cities in Brazil. Such cities are known as **primate cities**. In this case, they are much larger than the rank-size rule suggests.

The distribution of Brazil's major cities is very uneven (Figure 4). The cities are located mainly in the South-east and along the coast, the most densely populated and highly developed region of Brazil. Apart from river-port cities like Manaus on the Amazon, few cities grew up in the interior of Brazil. But this traditional pattern of urban growth is beginning to change with the development of new towns in the interior. The

◀ Fig 2
The growth of Brazil's five largest cities, 1872–1980.

urban societies differ from rural societies (see Table 1).
c Using the information in Figure 3 explain why many Brazilians migrate to large cities.

## Urban patterns

Like the development of the country as a whole, Brazil's urban population is concentrated in the big cities in the South-east. According to the **rank-size rule theory**, the size of a city is determined by its position or rank in the country's **urban hierarchy**. The rank-size rule states that the nth city in a hierarchy should be 1 nth of the size of the largest city. For example, the second largest city in Brazil, Rio de Janeiro, should be half the size of

São Paulo and the third largest city, Salvador, a third of the size. Table 2 shows how true or false this theory is in the case of Brazil's urban hierarchy.

| Few jobs apart from farming | Wide variety of jobs |
| Loss of jobs in farming (Machines do the work of men) | Many new jobs in industry |
| Few schools | Good educational opportunities |
| Few doctors | Higher standard of living |
| No hospitals | Good health services |
| Poor communications | Good communications |
| Low wages | Higher wages |
| Unfavourable image of countryside | Favourable city image – 'bright lights' |

RURAL 'PUSH'    URBAN 'PULL'

▲ Fig 3
The urban magnet. Note the 'push' and 'pull' factors.

construction of Goiana, the new state capital of Goiás in 1937, and the construction of the federal capital Brasilia in the interior in 1960 show how **government policy** can affect the distribution of major settlements.

## Profile of a Brazilian city

The structure of Brazilian cities is quite different from the structure of British cities (Figure 5). The city centre – Central Business District (CBD) – has modern, high-rise buildings. They are used for shops, offices and apartments for the well off. Most factory workers in Brazil need to live close to their work because they cannot afford transport.

*Table 2   Brazil's urban hierarchy*

| City | Actual population[1] | Rank-size rule population |
|------|---------------------|---------------------------|
| São Paulo | 7,033,530 | 7,033,530 |
| Rio de Janeiro | 5,093,232 | 3,516,765 |
| Salvador | 1,496,276 | 2,344,510 |
| Belo Horizonte | 1,442,483 | 1,758,382 |
| Recife | 1,184,215 | 1,406,706 |
| Brasilia[2] | 1,173,915 | 1,172,255 |
| Pôrto Alegre | 1,108,883 | 1,004,790 |
| Curitiba | 843,733 | 879,191 |
| Belém | 758,117 | 781,503 |
| Goiana | 703,263 | 703,353 |
| Fortaleza | 648,815 | 639,412 |
| Manaus | 613,098 | 586,127 |

[1] 1980 census figures
[2] Federal district

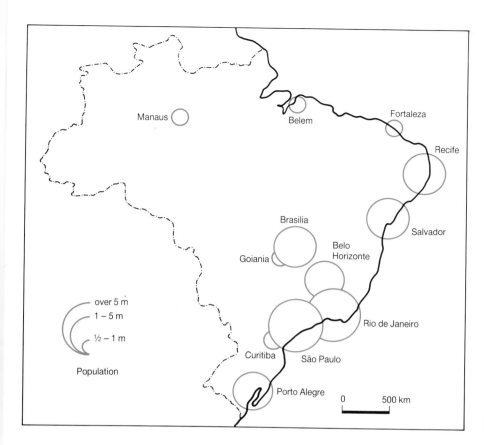

Fig 4 The distribution of Brazil's major cities.

b What TWO things do you notice about the distribution of cities in Brazil?

c What effect has government policy had on the location of cities in Brazil?

2 Briefly explain the following terms: (i) urban hierarchy; (ii) primate city.

3 In spite of the poverty in Brazil's favelas, living conditions in cities are generally better than in the country-side. Write a paragraph to support this view, using the data in Table 3.

4 Study Figure 5 carefully.

a Name the main land use zones in a typical Brazilian city.

b What do you think is the connection between urban land use and land values in a Brazilian city?

c How does the structure of a Brazilian city differ from the structure of a British city? If you have studied a British city at first-hand, use this as an example.

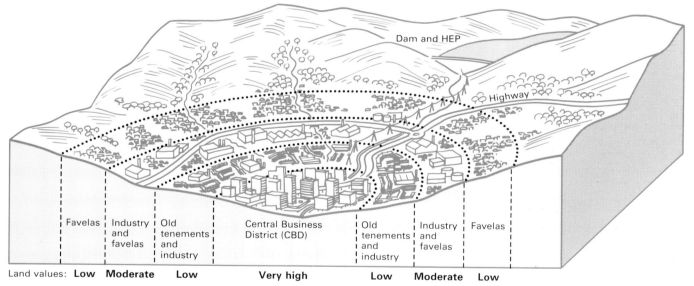

▲ Fig 5
Cross-section of a typical Brazilian city.

Consequently, housing and industry are often located in the same area, causing problems of pollution for the residents. In place of the middle class suburbs on the fringe of a British city there are favelas, housing the urban poor.

1 a How closely do the sizes of the following cities conform to the rank-size rule? (i) Rio de Janeiro; (ii) Brasilia; (iii) Fortaleza.

Table 3 Basic services and ownership of consumer goods in Brazil

|  | Percentage of households in 1980 | |
|  | Urban | Rural |
| --- | --- | --- |
| Electric light | 89 | 21 |
| Main water supply | 76 | 3 |
| Main sewerage | 38 | 8 |
| Radio | 79 | 68 |
| Refrigerator | 66 | 13 |
| Gas cooker | 83 | 13 |
| Television | 73 | 15 |
| Car | 28 | 9 |

# 20. Urban case studies

## São Paulo – a metropolitan giant

São Paulo is growing at an amazing rate. The skyline is continually changing because the city is growing so rapidly (Figure 1). Greater São Paulo occupies over 1,000 square kilometres – three times the size of the Isle of Wight – and is expanding by over 60 square kilometres annually. Its population now exceeds 11 million, more than Greater London which has nearly seven million inhabitants. São Paulo is growing by over half a million inhabitants a year (over 1,300 people a day), mainly with migrant families from other

► Fig 1
View of central São Paulo.

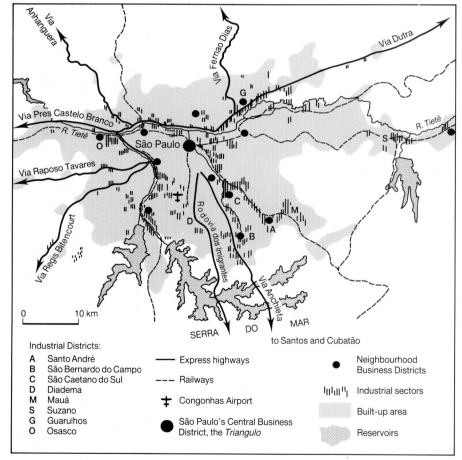

◄ Fig 2 Greater São Paulo.

regions of Brazil. In the past, many immigrants from European countries and Japan settled in São Paulo, swelling the population and making it a **multi-racial** or **cosmopolitan** city.

## São Paulo – an industrial giant

São Paulo has been described as 'the locomotive which pulls the rest of Brazil'. There is some truth in this saying, as São Paulo has become by far the largest city and the most important industrial centre in Brazil. Study Figure 2. How many **industrial districts** are there? There are over 25,000 industrial units in Greater São Paulo, from small workshops to large, modern factories (Table 1). The original stimulus for São Paulo's rapid growth came from the wealth of the coffee fazendas in São Paulo State. More recently it has been government policy to locate new high technology industries in the city. The advantages of locating industry in São Paulo include the excellent transport network, supplies of HEP from Cubatão and good access to Brazil's principal port at Santos (Figure 3).

1 a Using the information in Table 2, draw THREE pie graphs to represent the following data on São Paulo:

*Table 1   Typical industries in São Paulo*

| | |
|---|---|
| Textiles | Steel making |
| Food processing | Oil refining |
| Engineering | Petrochemical manufacturing |
| Metal working | Motor vehicle production |

*Table 2   São Paulo's importance as an industrial centre*

|  | São Paulo City | Greater São Paulo | São Paulo State |
|---|---|---|---|
| Factories | 12.5% | 15.7% | 30.7% |
| Industrial employment | 23.8% | 33.6% | 48.0% |
| Value of industrial production | 24.2% | 39.1% | 55.3% |

(All figures are a percentage of the Brazilian total)

▲ Fig 3
The Rodovia dos Imigrantes linking São Paulo and Santos.

▼ Fig 4
The Volkswagen car plant at São Bernardo do Campa.

(i) industrial employment in São Paulo City; (ii) value of industrial production in Greater São Paulo; (iii) number of factories in São Paulo State.

2 Find FOUR pieces of evidence in Figure 4 which indicate that São Bernardo do Campa is part of an industrial district.

3 Provide evidence to support each of the following statements about Greater São Paulo:
   a It is the largest metropolitan centre in Brazil.
   b It is a highly diversified industrial centre.
   c There are great contrasts in wealth in the city.

## Brasilia – capital of dreams

Brasilia is a dream come true. The idea of building a **federal capital** in the interior of Brazil dates back to the end of the eighteenth century. The site was over eight hundred kilometres from the well-populated south-east coastal region. The foundation stone was laid in 1922, and in 1960 the new capital city was officially opened. But from the outset, Brasilia has been a controversial development. The modern plan of the new capital was based on the shape of an aeroplane (Figure 5). The plan included **urban land use zones** for different functions. There are zones for residential buildings, government offices, and businesses. The central residential areas are called Super-Quadras or super-blocks. Each block is a self-contained building with flats, shops, schools, clubs and even cinemas. But the planners had not solved all the problems of big cities. While there is good accommodation for well-to-do middle and upper income families such as the civil servants who work in government offices, no plan was made for housing the low income labourers and their families. An estimated 600,000 people are still at work building this unfinished capital. They live in shanty towns and cheap housing in the so-called satellite areas outside the city (Figure 6). The original plan aimed at creating a kind of Venice in the city centre, with small streets and squares. These architectural details were never carried out because of the high cost. The centre is now carved up by wide roads, and there are large areas of waste land (Figure 7).

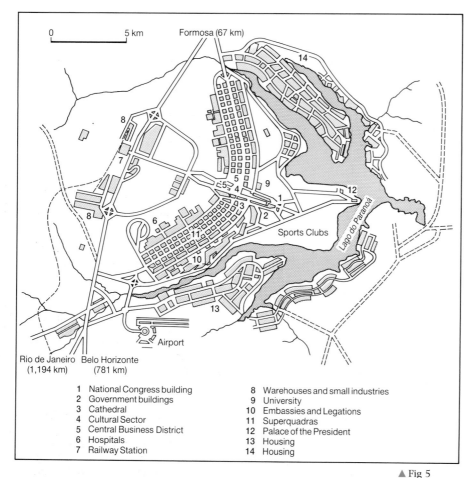

0    5 km    Formosa (67 km)

Lago do Paranoá

Sports Clubs

Airport

Rio de Janeiro    Belo Horizonte
(1,194 km)    (781 km)

| | | | |
|---|---|---|---|
| 1 | National Congress building | 8 | Warehouses and small industries |
| 2 | Government buildings | 9 | University |
| 3 | Cathedral | 10 | Embassies and Legations |
| 4 | Cultural Sector | 11 | Superquadras |
| 5 | Central Business District | 12 | Palace of the President |
| 6 | Hospitals | 13 | Housing |
| 7 | Railway Station | 14 | Housing |

▲ Fig 5
The layout of
Brasilia.

Certainly the expensive futuristic public buildings have done nothing to help solve the housing problem of low income families. But there is no doubt that Brasilia has succeeded as the new capital of Brazil. Since 1974, all government offices have moved from Rio de Janeiro to Brasilia (Figure 8). However, most employees return to Rio for their holidays. Moving the capital to the interior has also helped in the process of opening up Brazil and developing its valuable resources. The 'capital of dreams' is now a centre for economic development or **growth pole** and the focus of the road network in the interior. The city is a stepping stone to Brazil's frontier regions.

1 Why do you think Brasilia is called the 'capital of dreams'?
2 Imagine you are a Brazilian living in Rio de Janeiro. Make out two lists showing the advantages and disadvantages of moving to Brasilia.
3 Explain General Branco's dilemma over Brasilia when he came to power in 1964.
4 Design a brochure to attract people to Brasilia (i) as tourists or (ii) to work.

## Brasilia – urban pride or folly?

The total cost of the new capital city will never be known. It is also difficult to say whether the scheme has been worthwhile. Brazil could not afford its new capital city, so millions of dollars were borrowed from abroad. One president described Brasilia as an extravagant, anti-social waste of resources. After the military coup in 1964, the new President, General Branco, was faced with what he called 'the folly of finishing Brasilia and the crime of abandoning her'.

▼Fig 7
Brasilia – the city centre with offices and open space.

▼ Fig 6 The shanty town outside Brasilia which is home to the construction workers.

▼ Fig 8
The National Congress building in Brasilia. Find it on the map.

# 21. Towns for the poor

**Slums of hope**

Low cost homes for people with small incomes

Easy to build and maintain

Self-help communities

Major source of labour for industry

Improved opportunities for rural migrants

**Slums of despair**

Illegal

Unsafe, insanitary homes

Centres of vice and violence

High levels of unemployment

A 'sink' for the rural poor

An urban eyesore giving bad image of city

▲ Fig 1
Positive and negative views of favelas.

## The favelas

You will get a good idea of what a **favela** is like from Figure 1. It is a shanty town built by the urban newcomers, the rural migrants from other parts of Brazil. The favelas are one of the most striking features of Brazilian cities. Every major city has them, housing about a fifth of Brazil's urban population. The largest and oldest favelas like Jacarezinho in Rio de Janeiro are the size of large towns. That favela has over 32,000 residents. The large favelas occupy locations on the fringes of cities where there is plenty of available land. However, the most urgent need of the residents – the **favelados** – is money, so more often than not they build their shacks in smaller favelas on vacant land close to opportunities for work. They are found around the city centres, on building sites, by railways and factories – anywhere that offers some hope of employment.

1  What is the Brazilian name for (i) a shanty town and (ii) a person who lives in a shanty town?
2  There are positive and negative views about shanty towns. Study Figure 1 carefully.
   a  Describe in as much detail as possible the construction method and materials of a favela home.
   b  What attitudes do you think the following people would have towards the favela? (i) a local tourist office

manager; (ii) a town planner; (iii) a local church relief worker; (iv) a favelado.
3  Figure 2 is a model of rural migration and the development of favelas in a Brazilian city. Use this information to explain (i) why the population of favelas is growing and (ii) the size and location of favelas in different parts of the urban area.

## Life in the favelas

The sequence of pictures in Figure 3 shows some aspects of life in the Brazilian favelas. The land on which the favela is built is sometimes described as **marginal land** because it has little value. The site may be dangerous because of flood risk or

▼ Fig 2 Model of favela location and migration.

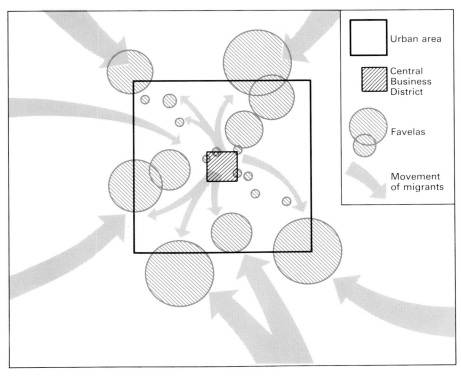

Urban area

Central Business District

Favelas

Movement of migrants

71

landslides, or it may be due for development. Either way, the favelados are usually regarded as illegal occupants by the authorities. The lack of basic services means there are serious health risks. Disease, like fire, spreads very quickly through the favelas. But in spite of the uncertainties of living in the favelas, many of them become thriving **self-help communities**, especially where the authorities have provided electricity and standpipes. Family incomes are very low, with the older children often helping out as wage-earners. But regular work is hard to come by. Even so, ambitions can run high in the favela because in contrast to life in the country, the city offers great hope.

▲ Fig 3a
A hillside favela. Why is this site dangerous?

▶ Fig 3b
A small favela in an industrial district of São Paulo. What is the advantage of this location?

▶ Fig 3d
A small favela in Recife. Why was this land not used for building?

◀Fig 3c
Note the building materials in this favela near a transport depot in São Paulo. Where do you think the materials come from?

▼Fig 3e
Children collecting water on a favela in Brasilia. Why do they need to do this?

1 Do you think it is more appropriate to call favelas slums of hope or slums of despair? Give your reasons.

2 Why do you think the future of the favelas is often uncertain?

3 a If you were given the task of improving life on a favela, what would you do to improve (i) housing conditions; (ii) people's health; (iii) family incomes?

  b What kind of problems might you encounter if you tried to carry out these improvements?

# 22. Regional planning

## Brazil's problem regions

In most countries the pattern of development is uneven. Usually, some regions, termed **core regions**, prosper while other regions may lag behind in their development (Figures 1 and 2). These backward or **peripheral regions** generally experience a combination of geographical disadvantages like harsh environments, poor communications, lack of resources and declining industries. To discover the extent of **regional inequality** in Brazil, look at Table 1. This table contains data on Brazil's five main regions. By comparing each region's share of population, wealth and other indicators of development we can begin to identify Brazil's problem regions.

▲ Fig 1
The core region: Modern housing in south-east Brazil.

◀ Fig 2
The periphery: A family of sharecroppers outside their home in north-east Brazil.

1 Identify (i) THREE signs of prosperity in Figure 1; (ii) THREE signs of backwardness in Figure 2.
2 Name Brazil's five planning regions (Figure 3).
3 Trace the map and pie graphs in Figure 4 (a) and (b) and use the information in Table 1 to complete them. Use a suitable method of shading and complete each of the keys. Add the heading 'Regional imbalance in Brazil'.
4 a Name the regions which you think make up the *core* and *periphery* of Brazil.
   b Which two regions do you think represent the *most developed* and *least developed* parts of Brazil?
   c Explain how you used information in Table 1 to answer (a) and (b).

◀ Fig 3

*Table 1    Patterns of development in Brazil*

| Regions | % Population | % National income | % Industrial production | % Industrial employment | % Cultivated farmland | % Forestry |
|---|---|---|---|---|---|---|
| North | 5 | 2 | 2 | 1 | 2 | 6 |
| North-east | 29 | 14 | 16 | 10 | 18 | 17 |
| Central-west | 6 | 3 | 5 | 2 | 25 | 10 |
| South-east | 44 | 64 | 55 | 70 | 33 | 14 |
| South | 16 | 17 | 22 | 17 | 22 | 53 |

Fig 4a

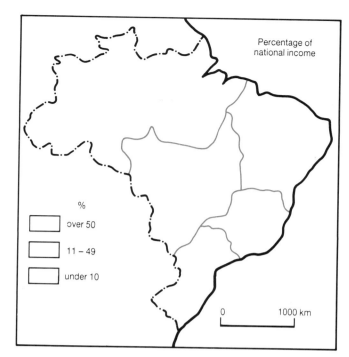

Percentage of national income

%
| | over 50 |
| | 11 – 49 |
| | under 10 |

0    1000 km

▲ Fig 6
The spiral of deprivation.

Lack of investment
Few new developments
Little advanced technology
Few jobs/high unemployment
Resources under-used
Low incomes
Migration out of region
Decline in local services
Aging workforce left behind
Lack of development/ stagnant economy

▼ Fig 4b

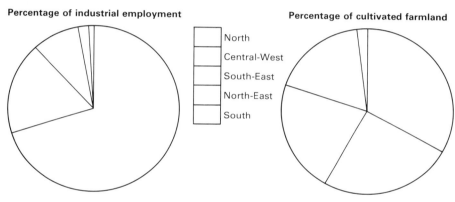

Percentage of industrial employment

Percentage of cultivated farmland

| | North |
| | Central-West |
| | South-East |
| | North-East |
| | South |

## A downward spiral

The Swedish economist Myrdal took a pessimistic view of regional development. He identified two kinds of change. The positive kind such as new industries and roads he called **spread effects**. They would help in the development of a region. But the spread effects would be off-set by negative influences, like migration from the region, which he called **backwash effects**. Myrdal's model shows a downward spiral of worsening conditions or **deprivation** in peripheral regions like north-east Brazil (Figure 6). According to this theory, the inequality between Brazil's regions would increase. The South-east would continue to develop at the expense of the North-east. The flow of migrants from the North-east into cities like São Paulo is evidence in support of Myrdal's theory. The work of SUDENE has not stopped migration from the region so far.

## Planning for development

In Brazil there are two major problem regions: the North-east and Amazonia. The Brazilian government has set up **regional development agencies** to tackle the social and economic problems of these regions: SUDAM (Superintendency for the Development of Amazonia) and SUDENE (Superintendency for the Development of the North-east). Funds were given to these agencies in order to develop agriculture and industry. In the case of Amazonia, the aim was to open up new land and resources in Brazil's vast frontier region. The main task for SUDENE was to break the vicious circle of poverty (Figure 5) and reduce the high rate of rural migration from the North-east.

▼ Fig 5
The vicious circle of poverty.

1  a  What is the effect of the vicious circle of poverty on development in North-east Brazil?
   b  What measures could be taken to break this vicious circle?
2  a  Name TWO examples of 'spread' effects and 'backwash' effects.
   b  Why is the 'backwash' effect hindering the development of north-east Brazil?
3  How is the Brazilian government planning to solve the country's regional problems?

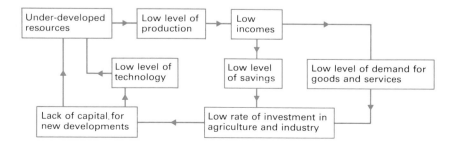

Under-developed resources → Low level of production → Low incomes → Low level of demand for goods and services

Low level of technology

Low level of savings

Lack of capital for new developments → Low rate of investment in agriculture and industry

75

# 23. North-east Brazil

## From wealth to poverty

The North-east was once the wealthiest part of Brazil. Its wealth came from a flourishing plantation economy. The main ports of Recife and Salvador were busy with overseas trade and a steady flow of immigrants seeking work in the colony. There was such a shortage of labour that thousands of slaves were brought in from Africa to work on the sugar plantations. That was over three hundred years ago. Now there is a different pattern of migration. Rural peasants and their families are leaving the countryside because there is no longer any work for them. They move to cities like Recife. Many families eventually migrate to more prosperous regions in the South-east. Today the North-east is a depressed, **underdeveloped region** (Figure 1). It is experiencing **economic decline** and **rural depopulation**. The fact is that the North-east has not shared in the rapid development of Brazil. It has 18 per cent of Brazil's land area, 29 per cent of the population and only 14 per cent of the national income. As well as poverty, the North-east has low living standards and levels of literacy. Look at the data in Table 1. The problems of the North-east arise mainly from **over-population** and poverty. Yet those living in the North-east also face an unfair land tenure system, the regular occurrence of chronic **droughts** and the lack of investment in new industries and the infrastructure (for example, roads and electricity).

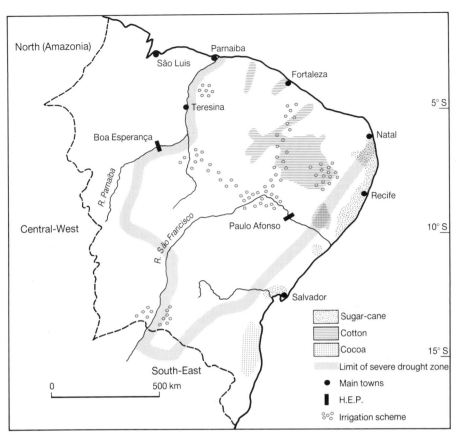

▲ Fig 1
North-east Brazil.

Table 1    Three symptoms of underdevelopment in the North-east region

|  | Household income[1] | Piped water[2] | Literacy[3] |
|---|---|---|---|
| **All areas** | | | |
| South-east | 13,925 | 65.9 | 79.3 |
| **NORTH-EAST** | **7,062** | **30.1** | **47.7** |
| Frontier | 10,808 | 38.2 | 63.3 |
| Brazil | 11,940 | 53.2 | 68.7 |
| **Rural areas** | | | |
| South-east | 8,589 | 3.9 | 65.1 |
| **NORTH-EAST** | **4,141** | **2.6** | **31.1** |
| Frontier | 8,459 | 2.8 | 48.3 |
| Brazil | 6,668 | 3.2 | 47.9 |
| **Urban areas** | | | |
| South-east | 16,593 | 82.6 | 83.4 |
| **NORTH-EAST** | **9,533** | **57.9** | **63.5** |
| Frontier | 13,323 | 61.9 | 74.1 |
| Brazil | 13,912 | 75.8 | 78.3 |

(Data is for 1980)
[1] Income in Cruzeiros (the Brazilian currency) per month.
[2] Piped water as a percentage of all households.
[3] Literacy rates for the population over 5 years of age, as a percentage.

# Some problems of the North-east

◀ Fig 2
Ruined crops. This farmer looks at the devastation caused by drought and insects. His family may be evicted soon – they have no title to the land.

▼ Fig 4
Sharecroppers cultivate land for an owner in exchange for a share of the harvest. These three are going to clear some land. They have to work very hard with simple tools. Most sharecroppers are extremely poor.

▶ Fig 3
A favela in Salvador, standing in marked contrast to middle class apartments. Rural migrants built the favela because they could not afford to buy or rent accommodation.

1 a Make THREE lists of problems in North-east Brazil under the headings: (i) physical problems; (ii) economic problems; (iii) social problems.

 b Figures 2–4 illustrate the problems facing three groups of people in North-east Brazil. Using evidence from these pictures, describe the problems each group faces in as much detail as possible.

2 a Draw THREE bar graphs to compare incomes, piped water and literacy in the North-east and the South-east regions of Brazil.

 b Using the evidence in your graphs, explain why many rural families from the North-east have migrated to urban areas in South-east Brazil.

3 The North-east has gone from being the most developed region in Brazil to being the most underdeveloped region. Write a paragraph explaining how this change has come about.

## Some solutions in the North-east

1 How do you think ordinary people living in the North-east have benefited from the kind of developments shown in Figures 5, 6 and 7?

2 The development agency SUDENE has been criticised for creating wealth but not work. What evidence can you see to support this view?

3 Write a short essay on one of the following statements:

a The North-east of Brazil is a nation within a nation.

b The North-east has become a stagnant backwater in the life of Brazil.

▲ Fig 5
A new hydroelectric power station on the São Francisco River. The power supplies will help in the industrial development of the North-east.

▲ Fig 6
Sugar-cane is a major product of North-east Brazil, but mechanisation has put many people out of work.

▶ Fig 7
Inside a plywood factory.

# 24. Amazonia

## The last frontier

Look at Figure 1. This family has recently arrived in Amazonia and cleared a site in the rainforest for crops and a hut. Like hundreds of other **colonists** in Amazonia, this family is struggling to make a living. They came under a government scheme to colonise and develop Amazonia. With the help of **multinational companies** the government has invested huge sums of money in development projects designed to open up the region and tap its natural resources. The plan, called *Polamazonia*, includes fifteen **growth poles** for economic development. The main types of development are shown in Table 1. Find the examples on the map of Amazonia in Figure 2. Some of these projects have already created a lot of wealth, especially for the companies in Amazonia. But many of them have

▼ Fig 2
Major projects in
Amazonia.

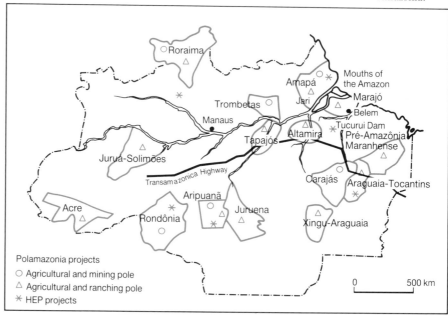

Polamazonia projects
○ Agricultural and mining pole
△ Agricultural and ranching pole
✳ HEP projects

led to the rapid destruction of the rainforest and the Indian way of life. Some experts predict that within a hundred years, the Amazon rainforests and Indian culture will have disappeared completely.

Table 1    *Major development projects in Amazonia*

| Project | Example |
|---|---|
| 1  Highway and feeder road construction | Transamazonica Highway |
| 2  Commercial agriculture and ranching | Juruena |
| 3  Lumbering and timber industries | Jari Project |
| 4  Open cast mining and refining industries | Carajás Iron Ore Field |
| 5  HEP production | Tucurui Dam |
| 6  Colonisation and settlement | Altamira, Rondônia |

## The environmental impact of projects

The impact of new projects on the environment of Amazonia has been severe. The seemingly endless rainforests were regarded as an obstacle in the way of economic development. There was little appreciation of the value of the rainforest environment and the need for conservation. Rondônia and Altamira are major colonisation projects in the heart of the Amazon rainforest (Figure 3). They consist of a new town or *agropolis* and small farms called *agrovilas* spread along the Transamazonica Highway. The plan

▲ Fig 3a
A new settlement in Amazonia: Rondônia.

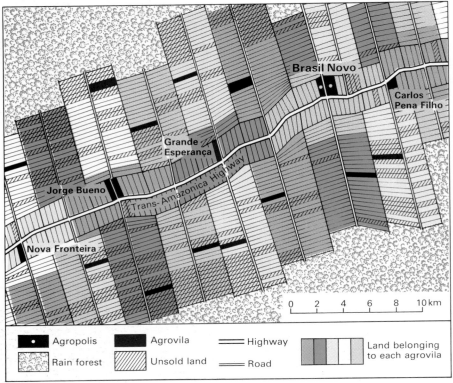

Brasil Novo

Carlos Pena Filho

Grande Esperança

Jorge Bueno

Trans-Amazonica Highway

Nova Fronteira

0  2  4  6  8  10km

■● Agropolis   ■ Agrovila   ═══ Highway   Land belonging to each agrovila
Rain forest   Unsold land   ─── Road

▲ Fig 3b
Plan of Altamira.

was to clear the rainforest in hundred-kilometre strips on either side of the road to make way for farming. However, the idea of exchanging the rainforests for productive farmland has not worked out. The colonists from the drought-stricken areas of the North-east were not experienced at farming in the rainforest. As harvests failed through soil infertility and erosion, migrant colonists often returned to their homes in other parts of Brazil.

The big cattle ranches and **agri-businesses,** averaging over 50,000 acres in size, were even more damaging to the environment. The effect of cutting down and burning

the forest and planting African grasses for pasture has been disastrous. (Figure 4.)

## Case study: The Jari Project

The Jari Project is located near the mouth of the Amazon River. The estate is about the size of Northern Ireland. The aim was to produce cellulose, plywood and veneers from quick-growing trees which were planted in place of the natural rainforest (Figure 5). The success of these industries has been followed by kaolin (china clay) mining, rice farming and cattle ranching. The farming is highly mechanised, using specially-adapted tractors and light aircraft for sowing and pest control. In addition, a new port has been constructed to handle exports from the estate. The project has created up to 100,000 jobs in farming and industry. There are community welfare services for workers and their

▼ Fig 4
The connection between deforestation and crop failure.

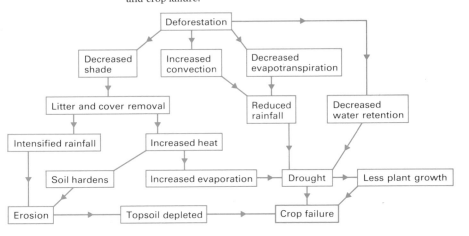

80

▲ Fig 5a
The Jari Project:
logging.

families on the estate. The Jari Project
is a success according to many
experts because it has combined
conservation with the creation of jobs
and wealth. The Jari Project has some
useful lessons for other parts of
Amazonia.

1 Explain how each project in Table 1
may lead to deforestation.
2 The attitude of many migrants from the
North-east changed once they had
been colonists in Amazonia for a few
years. Why do you think (i) they moved
to Amazonia in the first place and (ii)
some colonists are giving up farming in
Amazonia?
3 Make a list of reasons why the Jari
Project has been judged a success.
4 Using the information in Figure 4, give
THREE reasons why deforestation
leads to crop failure in Amazonia.

▲ Fig 5b
A cellulose mill; part
of the Jari Project.

## The human impact of
## projects

The rainforests of Amazonia are home
to some 50,000 Indians (Figure 6).
They live in small, scattered tribal
groups and depend on hunting,
fishing and farming for their survival.

▼ Fig 6
An Indian village in
Amazonia.

The development of roads and the rush for land in tribal hunting areas has brought about a major crisis for the Indians. For them, it was not only a question of '**culture shock**' as they came into contact with 'white' civilisation, often for the first time – their very survival was threatened.

Large-scale cattle ranching has taken its toll of Indian lives, mainly due to the transmission of western diseases.

We can say that development kills Indians. However, not all Indians have been killed. Some groups have succeeded in surviving in the face of tremendous pressures which have been put on them both physically and culturally.

Over half the population in four Yanomani villages died in a measles epidemic. The Indians had no natural immunity to this new disease and no innoculation against it.

The new highways have priority over the constitutional rights of the tribal people in government policy. It is calculated that the highways will violate more than 90% of the Indian population of Amazonia.

According to the colonial stereotype, the Indians were primitive, backward people who needed to be 'given shirts and civilised'. At best they were seen as 'noble savages'. This prejudiced attitude is giving way to a true assessment of Indian society and culture, from which white settlers have much to learn. In 1973 the Brazilian Minister of Health wrote: 'the tragedy is that the Indian is one of the main keys to the successful occupation of the Amazon, and as he disappears his vast wealth and knowledge is going with him.' The Indians know how to live in the rainforests without destroying them. Their livelihood has always depended upon conservation.

To help solve the problems Indians face, tribal reserves like the Xingu National Park have been set aside to give the Indians some protection from development in Amazonia (see Figure 2). They are administered by the National Indian Foundation (FUNAI). But the pace at which the Indians are being integrated into Brazilian society is increasing with the rapid economic development of Amazonia. Many Indians have already lost much of their original freedom. Now there is a further risk that they will become little more than a tourist attraction for the more adventurous visitors to Brazil.

1 If you were planning a documentary on the plight of the Brazilian Indians in Amazonia, what scenes would you include? (Describe three scenes).

2 a Separate or integrated? Discuss these alternatives for the Indians.

   b What do you think the long-term future of the Indians depends on? Give your reasons.

# INTERDEPENDENCE

# 25. Foreign trade

▲ Fig 1
Loading cellulose for export from the Jari Estate in Amazonia.

Over recent years the pattern of Brazil's foreign trade has changed. In particular, the 'economic miracle' – Brazil's rapid industrialization – has proved very costly. Modern technology from the USA, the European Community and Japan, and oil from the Middle East had to be imported. But Brazil's industrial policy has led to the development of **import-substituting industries** such as vehicle manufacture. Brazil no longer has to buy so many expensive manufactured goods like cars from abroad (Table 1). This kind of industry has helped Brazil's **balance of trade** by reducing the cost of imports and increasing the value of exports. However, until recently, the cost of imports greatly exceeded the value of exports, producing a massive **trade deficit** (Figure 2).

## The value of foreign trade

Shipping is one of Brazil's lifelines. The goods being loaded onto this ship (Figure 1) are **exports** which will earn Brazil valuable foreign currency. For Brazil, like the majority of countries, buying and selling goods abroad is an essential part of economic development. Brazilian coffee, for example, is sold throughout the world. At the same time, Brazil needs to buy products like oil from overseas. The money earned by exports like coffee helps to pay for **imports** such as oil. This exchange of products between countries is called **foreign trade**.

Value ($US billions)

Imports
Exports

7.0 6.2 — 1973
13.6 10.1 — 1975
13.2 12.1 — 1977

▼ Fig 2
Brazil's balance of trade.

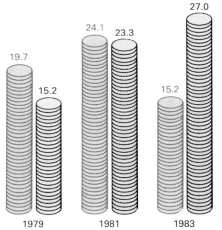

19.7 15.2 — 1979
24.1 23.3 — 1981
15.2 27.0 — 1983

### Table 1   Brazil's export trade in 1968 and 1982

|  | Percentage of all exports | |
|  | 1968 | 1982 |
| --- | --- | --- |
| *Primary products* | **79.5** | **40.3** |
| Coffee | 41.2 | 9.2 |
| Sugar | 5.4 | 1.2 |
| Cocoa | 2.5 | 1.1 |
| Iron ore | 5.6 | 8.8 |
| Soya beans | 1.3 | 8.5 |
| Others | 23.5 | 11.5 |
| *Manufactured products* | **20.5** | **59.7** |
| Semi-manufactured goods (e.g. pulp, pig iron) | 9.4 | 7.0 |
| Manufactured products (e.g. vehicles, footwear) | 10.6 | 51.4 |
| Others | 0.5 | 1.3 |

1 Using the information in Table 1, draw TWO pie graphs to show the primary and manufactured products exported in (i) 1968 and (ii) 1982. Provide a key to your graphs.

2 a What major changes in Brazil's export trade do your graphs indicate?

   b How do the exports in 1982 reflect Brazil's 'economic miracle'?

3 a Name the main economic activity represented in Figure 1.

   b Why is shipping described as one of Brazil's lifelines?

## The export quota system

Some developing countries are restricted in the amount of certain commodities they may export. Systems of **quotas** are used to allow all producers to have a share of the world market.

### Case study: Coffee quotas

Brazil belongs to the International Coffee Organisation. The ICO controls export quotas of coffee from major producers, of which Brazil is by far the largest. The price of coffee and the size of the quota is a major factor in the Brazilian economy (Figure 3).

▶ Fig 3 Handling sacks of coffee for export.

# A Full Quota of Troubles

Brazil, the world's biggest coffee producer, has a revolt on its hands, the scale of which can be measured by the way prices suffered one of their biggest ever falls in March.

Brazil's domination of the ICO came under attack from two sides – a group of eight producers and a handful of powerful consumers, among them the US. The group of eight – Costa Rica, the Dominican Republic, Ecuador, Peru, Papua New Guinea, Indonesia, Honduras and India – were fighting for a change in the distribution of ICO export quotas, the key to any effort to lift and stabilise world prices.

Prices, which collapsed to a near five-year low of $US1 per lb., have been playing havoc with the economies of those countries that rely on coffee as their main export earner.

The figures do show injustices, and explain the anger of those in revolt against Brazil, which enjoys a quota of 25.59% of exportable production. Those that lost out include Indonesia with a 7.26% slice of exportable production, India (1.22%) and Costa Rica (2.93%). Since small percentage differences one way or the other can mean losses or gains of millions of dollars, it is not difficult to see why the question of quota shares is seen as crucial.

(Adapted from an article in *South*, February 1987)

## Trade links

Brazil has trade links with most parts of the world. The European Community and the USA receive over half of Brazil's exports. Figure 4 shows the importance of these two regions for foreign trade, and the importance of the Middle East, which supplies most of Brazil's oil. The biggest change in the flow of Brazil's foreign trade is the increased trade with other less developed countries, including those in Latin America.

Between 1970 and 1980 Brazil's exports to other LDCs increased from nineteen per cent to thirty-six per cent, reflecting the competitive price of Brazilian goods in the poorer parts of the world.

## Economic interdependence

Foreign trade was worth over $US50,000 million to Brazil in 1986. Although this represents only a quarter of the value of trade in the UK, it made Brazil the world's seventeenth largest trading nation and the largest in the developing world. Brazil now relies heavily on world markets for its products. This makes it more **interdependent** within the world economic system. Brazilian products face stiff competition from developed countries and from other **newly industrialized countries** (NICs) like South Korea. At present the home market in Brazil is relatively small because wealth is very unevenly distributed amongst the population and wages are generally very low. Consequently Brazil will continue to rely on exports until demand for goods at home grows sufficiently to absorb a bigger share of its own production.

1 a How are the amounts of some commodity exports regulated for countries like Brazil?
  b Give TWO reasons why these regulations are made.
  c Why does the Brazilian government not want to reduce its coffee exports?
2 a What do the flow lines in Figure 4 represent?
  b How do they indicate Brazil's major trading partners?
  c Name FOUR trading partners according to the information on the map.
3 Explain the main reasons for Brazil's trade with the following regions: (i) USA; (ii) Middle East; (iii) EC; (iv) Other LDCs.

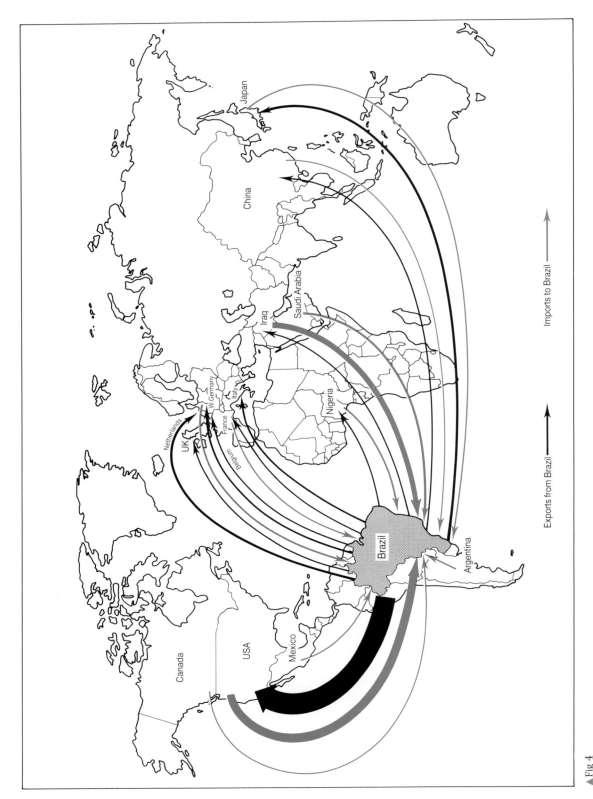

Canada

USA

Mexico

Japan

China

Saudi Arabia

Iraq

Netherlands
UK
W.Germany
France
Belgium
Italy

Nigeria

Brazil

Argentina

Exports from Brazil ⟶

Imports to Brazil ⟶

▲ Fig 4
Brazil's major
trading partners.

# 26. Overseas assistance

## Foreign aid

Development projects in Brazil are often paid for by other countries. Figure 1 shows an **aid project** in a slum district. Like most developing countries, Brazil receives development aid from overseas. The main source of aid is **official development assistance**. It consists of grants, loans and technical help from other governments and foreign banks. Most official development assistance must be paid for, usually with preferential terms such as low interest rates. It often has strings attached, restricting the aid to the purchase of goods in the **donor country**. Brazil also receives voluntary or **non-government aid** (NGA) from organisations like Oxfam, Christian Aid and the Catholic Fund for Overseas Development (CAFOD). This kind of aid focuses mainly on social and welfare projects. It does not have to be repaid.

While foreign aid has helped Brazil to develop, it has also increased its dependence on the outside world.

### Choosing an aid project

Aid donors are faced with choices. They must decide who should benefit from the project. In this activity you must decide what kind of aid project to support. Study the options in Figure 2 carefully.

**1** Which group of people is the aid intended to help?
**2** Name FIVE main kinds of aid project.
**3** Which TWO projects would, in your opinion, be the best way of providing aid? Justify your choices in as much detail as possible.

▲ Fig 1
Four years of accumulated rubbish are cleared from a slum in Salvador. The authorities do not provide refuse collection.

▼ Fig 2
Which course will aid the village poor?

|  | Guidance in self-help | Loans | Sponsorship | Direct gifts | Revolution |
|---|---|---|---|---|---|
| Aid | Salary for group organiser to help villagers to develop their own plans. | Loan for a diesel pump to provide drinking water from a well. | Monthly cash grants to provide food, health care and education. | Gift of sheep or cows to provide employment for poor families. | Moral support or weapons to liberate poor from oppressors |
| Advantages | Small outlay only. Possibility of permanent change in lives of the poor. | Contributes to health of villagers. Saves time and effort collecting water from river. | Raises some families above the poverty line. Provides donors with letters and information. | Income for a few families | Rapid results in changing the situation |
| Disadvantages | Requires skilled and sensitive organisers. Will be opposed by those with vested interests and needs legal aid. | Risk of non-repayment. Costs money to operate and maintain pump. Does not provide jobs. | High cost per head. Those children who are educated will probably leave village for the city | May develop the begging attitude and prevent farmers from helping themselves. Has little effect on village projects. | Backlash from authority. Possible sacrifice of lives. |

## Getting into debt

Brazil is one of many developing countries in debt (see page 8). The Brazilian government used loans from foreign banks to help finance its 'economic miracle'. The banks were prepared to lend large sums of money to Brazil because of the huge potential for industrial growth.

The new military government which had taken firm control of the country's economic development after the coup in 1964 was determined to achieve rapid economic growth at any price. But economic events elsewhere in the world during the 1970s caused severe problems in Brazil. The **world oil crisis** in 1974 hit Brazil very hard, as the price of imported oil rose more than four times in a single year. At the same time, international banks put up their **interest rates**. This meant that the cost of borrowing went up. The world **recession** that followed effectively reduced Brazil's export trade because developed countries like Britain cut back on imports. Brazil had the world's largest **debt burden**, having borrowed over $US104 billion in 1985 (Figure 3). As early as 1980 Brazil was borrowing money from abroad just to repay the interest on its loans. Brazil's **foreign debt** represented 3.4% of the Gross National Product and interest repayments alone amounted to $US4,142 million. As a result of the debt burden, the Brazilian government was forced to abandon its policy of growth at any price and take action to deal with the problem (Table 1).

1 a Name TWO major kinds of foreign aid.
  b What is the main difference between these kinds of aid?
2 a Give THREE reasons why you think that foreign governments and banks were willing to make large loans to Brazil.
  b Referring to Figure 3 explain how (i) the total debt and (ii) the rate of debt growth changed between 1973 and 1987.
  c What international events brought about Brazil's massive debt problem?

3 a Study Table 1. Put the areas of expenditure in order of importance according to how effective you think the measures will be.
  b Give reasons for the two areas of expenditure you selected as being most effective and least effective.

## Voluntary assistance

Voluntary organisations like Christian Aid, CAFOD and Oxfam generally support community projects which are aimed at getting people to help themselves. These aid organisations support community health and education programmes, neighbourhood associations working against poverty and small-scale agricultural and fisheries projects where the aim is to improve food production and diets. By providing this kind of assistance at the 'grass roots' level the voluntary organisations can begin to tackle the problems facing ordinary people in their everyday lives (Figure 4).

### Case study 1: Women's health

'*The Day of a Woman* is a video film about the favela women of Recife and their most pressing problems. It is just one of the education projects begun by SOS Corpo, a health group working with women and young people in the poor districts of the city.

The problems of poverty such as inadequate housing, lack of sanitary facilities and of clean water affect everyone, but women bear an extra burden: they have to care for children and provide for the needs of the family.

During repeated migrations from one part of the country to another in search of work, families are often broken up. Women tend to be left alone to feed and care for several children with the scarce resources earned through domestic service or occasional labour.

Set up in 1980, SOS Corpo has concentrated its education work among poor women. Helped by a £10,524 grant from Christian Aid, SOS Corpo commissioned seven videos on subjects including childbirth and pregnancy, medical provision in the Recife area, the government's health programme and the everyday life of women.'

(Adapted from the Christian Aid sheet 'Focus on Brazil')

▼Fig 3
Brazil's debt burden.

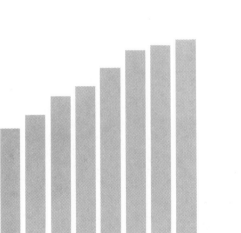

Table 1   *Reducing the debt burden*

| Areas of expenditure | Action |
| --- | --- |
| Imports | Reduce cost of goods bought from overseas. |
| Energy | Cut down on imported oil by developing alternative sources of energy. |
| Wages | Hold down wages to keep prices low and competitive. |
| Credit | Control credit and reduce costly interest payments. |
| Government spending | Cut government spending on projects likely to be expensive. |
| Foreign debt | Reschedule foreign debts and spread repayments over a longer period of time. |

▲Fig 4
A supply of clean
water reduces
disease in a favela.

▼Fig 5
A community
housing project in
São Paulo.

## Case study 2: A Community housing programme

'One of the major problems facing people in shanty towns is insecurity. Families who have no option but to build their tin and cardboard shacks on any spare plot of land often suffer harsh consequences. Shanty towns can disappear in a single day, knocked down by bulldozers. Families are left homeless once again. In São Paulo, CAFOD is helping the poor in three slum areas to establish their rights to the plots of land on which their huts stand. The communities plan to buy a brick-making machine so that, once they have security of tenure on their homes, they can start constructing more solid, permanent homes (Figure 5).

CAFOD has approved a grant of £3,000 towards the legal costs involved in establishing ownership.'

(Adapted from the CAFOD Development Programme in Brazil).

1 Make a list of the benefits brought by voluntary organisations in the two case studies.

2 In 1984 the official minimum wage in Brazil was £26 a month. With inflation running at around 200%, this wage packet was worth only £22 in the shops. At the same time there were high levels of unemployment and underemployment, with people in temporary jobs. The situation has not improved.

  a How is the above information reflected in the housing situation?

  b If you were the minister responsible for housing and social welfare in Brazil, what action would you take in order to reduce the problem of poverty?

  c Briefly explain what effect your recommendations would have on the problems of poverty and poor housing.

3 Given Brazil's current economic policies and problems, what do you think the poor of Brazil can hope for in the way of improved living standards?

# 27. Tourism

## Brazilian Blend

**Day 1  London to Rio.** Departure from London Heathrow by Varig. Direct to Rio de Janeiro.

**Day 2  Rio.** Morning arrival in Rio. Transfer to Hotel Copacabana Palace. Remainder of day at leisure.

**Days 3 and 4  Rio.** Now that you have had time to relax after your long flight you can now begin to discover the sights of this fantastic city. Included in your stay is a cable car ride to the top of Sugar Loaf Mountain and a trip to the Corcovado where you join the Statue of Christ to survey the city from over 2,000 feet.

**Day 5  Rio to Manaus.** A morning flight from Rio to Manaus. Transfer to the Hotel Tropical set in the heart of the Amazon Jungle, on the river bank of the Rio Negro. The hotel offers superb amenities and every comfort. Brief sightseeing in the city of Manaus includes the market place, the Amazon Theatre and Indian Museum.

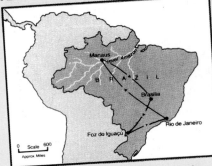

**Day 6  Manaus.** Full day excursion by small boat on the Rio Negro through almost untouched nature as we penetrate the myriad of 'igarapes' and 'igapos' (small creeks). A regional lunch will be served in the house of a 'caboclo'.

**Day 7  Manaus.** A free day in Manaus to enjoy more sightseeing or relax in the tranquility of your hotel.

**Day 8  Manaus to Brasilia.** The afternoon flight from Manaus brings you to Brasilia, futuristic capital city of Brazil. In 1960 the architect Oscar Niemeyer had his dream realised and this space age city was born. The night will be spent at the comfortable Carlton Hotel.

**Day 9  Brasilia.** Our morning city tour will introduce you to the almost science-fictional modern beauty of Brasilia. Enjoy the rest of the day at leisure.

**Day 10  Brasilia to Foz do Iguacu.** More time for relaxing or sightseeing in Brasilia, before your evening flight to Iguacu. Transfer from the aiport to the Hotel Das Cataratas (sister hotel to the Tropical) and one which enjoys the commanding location in front of the famous falls.

**Day 11  Iguacu.** "The Festival of Waters" Iguacu falls, a show without intervals. For many people the highlight of their tour of Brazil. 275 separate cataracts and falls pour millions of gallons of water every second, into the foaming river below. The Parque Nacional Do Iguacu, surrounding the falls, offers glorious walks through sub tropical jungle alive with exotic birds and flowers.

**Day 12  Iguacu.** Enjoy further the sights and sound of the falls, or take an optional excursion to Paraguay or Argentina.

**Day 13  Iguacu to Rio.** A chance to relax before your evening flight back to Rio and the Copacabana Palace Hotel.

**Days 14 to 15  Rio.** Now there is the opportunity to further explore this most flamboyant and glamorous of South American cities. Optional excursions by night and days include Plataforma 1 or Scala nightclubs, or half day trip to Petropolis, the mountain town once the home of Emperor Pedro II. The speciality restaurant of Brazil is the Churrascarias (barbeque), although most international tastes are catered for. Rio is an exciting place to shop for precious stones, Indian goods, leather, fashionable beach wear and, of course, coffee. Whatever your holiday mood, Rio has something to please.

**Day 16.** Depart from Rio de Janeiro for London Heathrow.

▲Fig 1
Sixteen days in paradise?

### Beautiful Brazil

'Visit breathtaking Brazil'; 'See paradise for yourself'. This is the language of tourist brochures. Figure 1 shows the sixteen-day holiday offered by one holiday company. Their brochure creates an impression of tropical luxury and the 'once in a lifetime' holiday most of us can only dream about (Figure 2).

Brazil has an enormous potential for **tourism**. The main attractions are cultural and scenic, but remoteness from the main cities and airports prevents most tourists from seeing many of Brazil's most striking natural features. Figure 2 shows what you would miss if you did not visit the north and west of the country.

The government's policy of opening up the interior is helping with the expansion of tourism. The city of Manaus, which is about four days up the Amazon by river boat, became run-down after the rubber boom era. Now Manaus has been made a **free port**, with duty-free trading and tax incentives for companies, and so has become the centre for tourism in Amazonia.

1  Make a list of as many tourist attractions as you can from the information in the brochure (Figure 1). Divide these attractions into two groups: (i) city life; (ii) natural scenery.
2  Describe some typically Brazilian souvenirs you could buy on this holiday.
3  Using the information in Figure 2, describe the main attractions for tourists wanting to visit Amazonia.
4  Why do you think Rio de Janeiro is the most popular tourist centre in Brazil?
5  a  What are the main tourist attractions in your home region?
   b  In what ways do you think the tourist attractions of Brazil and your home region are (i) similar and (ii) different?

### The sunshine industry

Brazil, like many other developing countries, is turning to tourism as a means of earning foreign currency. Although Brazil is a long way from the centres of mass tourism in the USA and Western Europe, it attracts tourists from many parts of the world (Figure 4). Now the government is taking steps to promote Brazil's tourist image through its national tourist authority, Embratur. It aims to make Brazil an alternative attraction to traditional tourist centres such as Hawaii and the Caribbean.

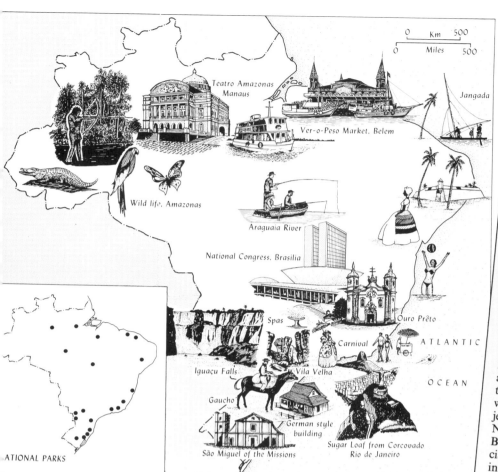

▲ Fig 2
Tourist images of
Brazil.

NATIONAL PARKS

## Case study: Embratur

Brazil was discovered by the Portuguese navigator Pedro Cabral in 1500 by mistake – he was bound for the East Indies! Today Brazil is making a deliberate effort to be rediscovered, this time by tourists. Brazil, or more accurately Rio, has always been a haunt of the upper-income jet-setter, flying in for the Carnival and a quick samba. Embratur has made a conscious effort to attract the middle-income traveller from beyond South America. Varig, the main Brazilian airline, increased the size of its fleet, expanded its network and now operates regular charter flights from Canada, USA, West Germany and Switzerland. Embratur's most noted promotional effort has been the Brazil Air Pass. Valid on all Brazilian airlines, the pass can be bought anywhere in the world. The idea has been a success both for the tourist and for Brazil. Before the Air Pass was available, 57% of all tourists came just to Rio. The launching of the service was the crucial link in Embratur's project to promote new areas like the North-east, Amazonia and southern Brazil. The government offered financial incentives to companies investing in ventures such as the construction of hotels, marinas and wildlife parks. Five convention centres have been built in Rio, São Paulo, Recife, Brasilia and Salvador, accommodating between 2,000 and 8,000 in a bid to persuade businessmen to meet in Brazil.

(Adapted from an article in *The Financial Times*, 5 November 1984)

◀ Fig 3
Carnival in Rio de
Janeiro.

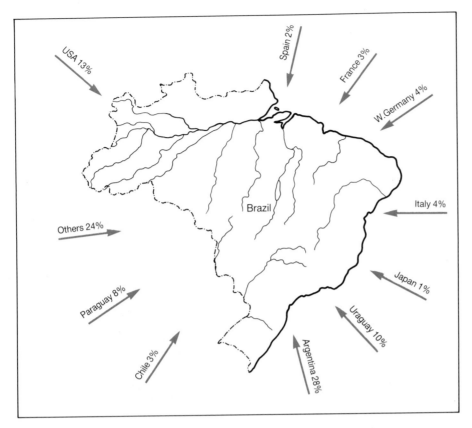

▲ Fig 4
Where Brazil's
tourists come from.

However, Brazil has not yet made it as a big-time tourist attraction like Spain or Britain (Table 1). The industry suffers from Brazil's isolation and the high cost of travel from other parts of the world.

1 What is another name for the 'sunshine industry'?
2 What do you think is meant by (i) mass tourism and (ii) traditional tourist centres?
3 Describe the different ways the Brazilian tourist industry is being developed.
4 a From Figure 4 name the FOUR main origins of tourists in Brazil.
  b Why do you think relatively few British tourists go on holiday to Brazil?

## Who gains from tourism?

In 1982 Brazil earned over $US1,608 million from tourism. It is spending millions of dollars on its **tourist infrastructure**. For example, air-conditioned hotels, airports, entertainment facilities and specialist facilities like yacht marinas and wildlife parks are being provided to encourage tourism. In Rio de Janeiro, shanty towns in 'high profile' areas are pulled down to prevent tourists getting negative impressions of the country. The bankers, tour operators and hoteliers do well from tourism. However, the tourist industry in Brazil underlines the social and economic division of the country into 'haves' and 'have-nots'. As an industry, tourism offers nothing to the 'have-nots' of Brazil, unless of course you count the growing amount of begging and scavenging in the tourist centres like Rio.

1 Refer to Table 1.
  a How important is Brazil as a tourist destination compared with (i) Britain; (ii) Spain; (iii) Egypt?
  b What evidence can you find in Figure 4 and Table 1 to support the view that tourists in Brazil are 'big spenders' from relatively wealthy countries in comparison with tourists in other developing countries?
2 There are different attitudes towards tourism and tourists in Brazil. Here are three:
  *Tour operator.* 'We like to keep our customers away from the shanty towns. They are not what visitors come to see in Brazil.'
  *American tourist.* 'It's fantastic! The climate, the hotel, the beach, the night-life. And what about those little children begging. Aren't they just cute!'
  *A favelado:* 'We have little to do with rich tourists. They spend lots of money here in Rio, but it just goes into the pockets of rich Brazilians.'
Explain why you think these people have different views about tourism.

Table 1   Top twenty for tourism in the developing world, 1982

| Rank | Country | Number of tourists | Revenue ($USM) |
|---|---|---|---|
| 1 | China | 7,900,000 | 840 |
| 2 | Mexico | 4,145,000 | 1,670 |
| 3 | Singapore | 2,947,000 | 1,916 |
| 4 | Hong Kong | 2,302,000 | 1,317 |
| 5 | Thailand | 2,218,000 | 972 |
| 6 | Malaysia | 2,093,000 | 357 |
| 7 | Jordan | 2,076,000 | 510 |
| 8 | Iraq | 2,020,000 | 54 |
| 9 | Bahamas | 1,947,000 | 688 |
| 10 | Morocco | 1,815,000 | 333 |
| 11 | Puerto Rico | 1,679,000 | 615 |
| 12 | Turkey | 1,625,000 | 411 |
| 13 | Tunisia | 1,438,000 | 600 |
| 14 | Egypt | 1,423,000 | 562 |
| 15 | India | 1,288,000 | 800 |
| 16 | S. Korea | 1,145,000 | 502 |
| 17 | Colombia | 1,127,000 | 624 |
| 18 | Argentina | 1,120,000 | 344 |
| 19 | Brazil | 1,100,000 | 1,608 |
| 20 | Venezuela | 1,003,000 | 246 |
| | Spain | 40,129,000 | 6,970 |
| | Great Britain | 11,500,000 | 3,850 |

# 28. Growth or development?

◀ Fig 1
The Petrobras oil refinery at Cubatão. What problems do people living here face?

▶ Fig 2
In a wealthy city, why do these people have to sleep on the pavement?

## Who is development for?

What do Figures 1 and 2 tell you about development in Brazil? Would you wish to live in these conditions? The fact is that the main goal of the Brazilian development strategy is economic growth. The government measures progress towards this goal in terms of wealth. The indicators of this progress include the Gross National Product (GNP) and productivity from the major sectors of the economy – agriculture, mining, industry and services. The problem is that economic growth in Brazil excludes social development and the welfare of many people. The poor and **minority groups** like the Indians, for example, have not benefited from Brazil's 'economic miracle'. For the Indians, the development of Amazonia has been disastrous. Many peasant families have also experienced so-called agricultural development only to lose their livelihood. Economic growth and development are not one and the same thing.

1 Using the evidence in Figures 1 and 2, how would you answer the questions in the captions?
2 Explain the difference between economic growth and development. Use information about the 'economic miracle' and minority groups to illustrate your answer.

## Development and the environment

People depend upon their environment. It provides them with their means of existence – air, water and food. Without these **resources** people would be unable to survive.

93

In parts of Brazil the environment is now under serious threat from economic activities. In the large industrial cities, the air is so polluted that it causes disease, especially in the very young. The rivers and soils become so poisoned that they are often unusable. In rural Brazil huge **dams** and **agribusinesses** are eating up forest and farmland at an alarming rate. The dams are being built to hold back rivers for HEP projects. The lakes created by these dams are flooding vast tracts of land once inhabited and farmed. Agribusinesses, too, are taking over more and more of Brazil's forests and farmland. These big businesses also buy up smallholdings and bring in labour-saving machines. The villagers lose their land and their means of survival so they usually migrate to the cities, ending up in a favela, without work or money.

Dams and agribusinesses represent progress. They provide power for industry and increased production of meat and cash crops. The wealth created by economic development is mainly used for paying off debts to international moneylenders like the World Bank. So Brazil is caught in a **vicious circle** of economic growth and debt. It does not pay for clinics to deal with diseases spread by pollution and water-borne parasites living in the newly-created lakes. It does not

provide alternative employment for villagers displaced by lakes or made landless by big business. It does not pay for better homes and improved living conditions for the urban and rural poor who make up about a third of Brazil's population.

## Two Brazils

Brazil's growth policies have left the country and its people divided. For the 'haves' living in the more developed parts of Brazil the gains of economic growth have been little short of miraculous. But those in less developed parts of Brazil now require a miracle to help them escape the consequences of uncontrolled growth. As always, it is the poorer people who experience the consequences of deteriorating environmental conditions first. For Brazil, the main tasks for development should be providing a fairer distribution of wealth and resources and conserving the environment.

1 Draw up arguments for use in a debate on the development of Brazil, using the example of a major HEP project. The motion for the debate is 'Dams are good for industry so they are good for Brazil'. Write down arguments both for and aganst the motion.

If there is an opportunity, hold the debate in class. Note the conclusions of the debate and the final vote.

## The limits to growth

What happens if industry, population and cities grow unchecked? A best-selling book called *The Limits to Growth* came up with a gloomy forecast (Figures 3 and 4). The key to this **model of growth** is the balance between diminishing resources and growing population. There are no values on the vertical scale as the graphs show general trends for each variable. It is easy to see why the forecast is gloomy by comparing the relationship between population and resources, first in 1900 and then in the year 2100.

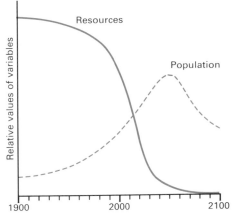

▲ Fig 3
The limits to growth: resources and population.

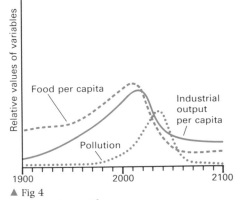

▲ Fig 4
The limits to growth: food, pollution and industrial output.

1 a Trace Figures 3 and 4 on to a single graph. Label your graph The Limits to Growth model.
  b Name the FIVE variables used in the model.
  c Describe the major changes that are predicted.
2 Explain why the Limits to Growth model is sometimes described as a forecast of gloom and doom.

---

## Case study: Pollution is bad for your health

Rapid, uncontrolled industrial and urban growth has left São Paulo with many problems. There are many shanty towns which reflect the lack of

adequate housing for the poorer people of the city. Around major industrial complexes there is serious **pollution**. The passage below describes the problems facing the people of nearby Cubatão.

One region, Cubatão, has been dubbed 'The Valley of Death'. Just an hour away from São Paulo's chic downtown area, Cubatão is the home of Latin America's biggest petrochemical complex. Vila Parisi is a crowded Cubatão slum with 15,000 residents. The town is boxed in on its four sides by a steel plant, a fertilizer factory, a cement works and a mountain wall. There are about 30 major industrial facilities in the vicinity. The slum, which lies below sea-level, experiences severe and frequent flooding when the open sewers overflow into the muddy streets. The local rivers are laced with toxic waste, detergents and other industrial pollutants. A 1981 study found that the residents of Vila Parisi lived under a barrage of air pollutants: 473 tons of carbon monoxide, 182 tons of sulphur, 148 tons of polluted dust and particles and 41 tons of nitrogen oxide every day. Doctors who examined members of the Vila Parisi population in 1983 found that 44% had some kind of lung disease. The infant mortality rate in Cubatão is significantly higher than anywhere else in the country.

(Adapted from an article by R. Kazis in the *New Internationalist*, 3/1986)

# Data Base

**Wealth and economic development**

| | GNP/CAP ($US) | Av. annual Growth of GNP/CAP 1965–85 | %GDP from services | Energy consumption per cap (kg of oil equiv.) |
|---|---|---|---|---|
| Brazil | 1,640 | 4.3 | 54 | 781 |
| India | 270 | 1.7 | 41 | 201 |
| Nigeria | 800 | 2.2 | 32 | 165 |
| UK | 8,460 | 1.6 | 62 | 3,603 |
| Canada | 13,680 | 2.4 | 67 | 9,224 |

**Economic dependence**

| | Exports/CAP ($US) | Official aid ($US M) | Aid as a % of GNP | Foreign debt as a % of GNP |
|---|---|---|---|---|
| Brazil | 189 | 123 | 0.1 | 35.5 |
| India | 13 | 1,470 | 0.7 | 13.5 |
| Nigeria | 126 | 32 | 0.04 | 17.2 |
| UK | 1,789 | nil | nil | nil |
| Canada | 2,889 | nil | nil | nil |

**Population change**

| | Av. annual % growth rate 1980–85 | Birth rate per 1,000 population | Death rate per 1,000 population | Life expectancy male/female |
|---|---|---|---|---|
| Brazil | 2.3 | 29 | 8 | 62/67 |
| India | 2.2 | 33 | 12 | 57/56 |
| Nigeria | 3.3 | 50 | 16 | 48/52 |
| UK | 0.1 | 13 | 12 | 72/77 |
| Canada | 1.1 | 15 | 7 | 72/80 |

**Health and well-being**

| | Infant mortality per 1,000 pop. | Daily calorie supply | Population per doctor | Population per hospital bed |
|---|---|---|---|---|
| Brazil | 67 | 2,633 | 1,632 | 245 |
| India | 89 | 2,189 | 2,545 | 1,265 |
| Nigeria | 109 | 2,038 | 9,591 | 1,307 |
| UK | 9 | 3,131 | 711 | 127 |
| Canada | 8 | 3,432 | 548 | 129 |

**Modernisation**

| | TV sets per 1,000 pop | % population living in urban areas | % 20–24 age group in higher ed. | % of adults illiterate |
|---|---|---|---|---|
| Brazil | 126 | 73 | 11 | 24 |
| India | 1 | 25 | 9 | 64 |
| Nigeria | 5 | 30 | 3 | 75 |
| UK | 394 | 92 | 20 | 1 |
| Canada | 466 | 77 | 44 | 1 |

**Transport and communications**

| | Passenger cars per 1,000 population | Railways km/10,000 population | Telephones per 1,000 population | Daily newspapers per 1,000 population |
|---|---|---|---|---|
| Brazil | 5 | 2.4 | 63 | 126 |
| India | 7 | 0.9 | 4 | 20 |
| Nigeria | 3 | 0.4 | 14 | 6 |
| UK | 25 | 3.1 | 477 | 453 |
| Canada | 42 | 2.7 | 686 | 241 |

# Index